"Lost in the political and economic challenges/upheavals and violence that threaten society at the national and global scenes, most people seldom look down and around them to perceive a worse crime that scourge humanity – Domestic Violence. Sr. Helen Ogbuji in her beautifully and lucidly articulated book draws our attention to the ravages of this monster that dwells among us. *Dealing Effectively with Domestic Abuse* very importantly is largely a fruit of the author's ministerial experience that does not end at exposing the cruelty of Domestic Abuse in Africa but proffers universally praxis-based solutions. The application of the theological concept of reconciliation is uniquely *ad rem*. The thrust that genuine reconciliation precedes true healing is empowering to abused persons and transforming to the social structures that bolster violence. *Dealing Effectively with Domestic Abuse* is a handy tool for all in ministry, both ordained and non-ordained. It is a *'must read'* for all men and women in relationships especially those facing abuse in their relationships. As an advocate of empowerment and emancipation of abused persons, I found the book enriching."

– Rev. Fr. Dr. Henry Ogbuji, author of *From Where Shall Come Our Help? The Lament of Abused Persons*

"This book is appropriate for families who are finding it difficult to come out from their debased life of hatred, violence, and unforgiving heart… It is valid for formators, educators, and those who journey with the vulnerable people as it offers relevant perspectives for an approach to interpreting the domestic life situation in general and the steps to move towards healing and reconciliation. I recommend this book to everyone because we all come from families."

– Sr. Dr. Elizabeth Ngozi Okpalaenwe, MSHR

"A refreshing and reshaping text. Sister Helen invites carefully but energetically to compassionate relations among Christians–the core of our faith: forgive as you breathe. Must read for all concerned leaders."

– Rev. Dr. Emmanuel Foro, SJ

"Violence in our society is the antithesis of what it means to be human, and to live like one. Sr. Adaku, in this well-researched and finely articulated book, adds to the moral voice of awareness, caution, and solution. I do recommend this book to those who seek enlightenment and desire to stop domestic violence."

— Rev. Udo Ogbuji, author of *The Peace I Know*

"Sr. Adaku's work in this text is a testimony of hope and compassion. Grounded in faith, she believes in the power of the Risen Christ to undo all the wrongs of violence inflicted on the innocent. The book seeks to be a concrete expression of God's love directed towards those most in need of healing from domestic violence."

– Sr. Collen Mary Mallon, OP, PhD

Sr. Adaku Helen Ogbuji, CCVI, Ph.D.

Dealing Effectively with Domestic Abuse

The Ministry of Reconciliation and Healing

En Route Books and Media, LLC
Saint Louis, MO

En Route Books and Media, LLC
5705 Rhodes Avenue
St. Louis, MO 63109

Contact us at **contact@enroutebooksandmedia.com**

Cover Credit: Dr. Sebastian Mahfood, OP, using dreamstime.com

Copyright 2015, 2024 Sr. Adaku Helen Ogbuji, CCVI, Ph.D.

First published by CUEA PRESS
Catholic University of Eastern Africa, Nairobi, Kenya

ISBN-13: 979-8-88870-178-2
Library of Congress Control Number: 2024948677

All rights reserved. No part of this book may be reproduced, stored in a retrieval system, or transmitted in any form, electronic, mechanical, photocopying, or otherwise, without the author's prior written permission.

Dedication

This work is dedicated to the Sacred Heart of the Incarnate Word, overflowing with compassionate love for the suffering.

Table of Contents

Acknowledgments v

Foreword vii

Preface ix

Definition of Terms xi

Introduction 1
    Case 1 2
    Case 2 5

Chapter 1: The Meaning of Domestic Violence with the
    Experiences of African Women 15
    Different Faces of Abuse 24
    Widowhood Practices and Rituals in Nigeria 42
    Effects of Abuse on Children 44
    Catalyst of Domestic Violence 48

Chapter 2: The Church's Teaching on the Dignity of Women 59
    The Theology of the Body (TOB) 65

Chapter 3: Toward a Genuine Reconciliation Process 69
    Meaning of Genuine Reconciliation 71
    Relationship between Reconciliation and Violence 74
    The Ineffective Methods of the Reconciliation Process 82

Reconciliation as a Hasty Peace 84
Reconciliation Instead of Liberation 87
Reconciliation as a Managed Process.. 90
The Process of True Reconciliation 93
Using the Right People... 94
Using the Right Approach 95
The process of releasing the pain of abuse: 98
Right Timing 101

Chapter 4: Genuine Healing through the Process of Reconciliation
.... 105
Healing – Physical, Emotional, and Spiritual............................ 107
What Forgiveness Does in the Healing Process........................ 110
The Role of the Church in the Healing Process 115
The Healing Message of the Gospel.. 116
The Healing of the Canaanite Woman's Daughter in Matthew 15:21-28 118
Jesus and the Crippled Woman in Luke 13:10-17.................... 121
The Encounter of Jesus with the Samaritan Woman in John 4:1-42 126
The commonality of these Stories and their Application........ 129
The Power of Ritual in the Healing Process 135

Chapter 5: Recommendations 140
Formulation of Prayer against Domestic Violence.................. 141

Table of Contents

    Pastoral Letter from the Bishops 142

    Interpretation of the Scripture using the Lens of Jesus 144

    Formation of Solidarity Groups for Women in the Society ... 146

    The Church and the Civil Authorities 149

Conclusion 152

Bibliography 158

Acknowledgments

I am grateful to God for the opportunity to complete this work. I acknowledge the spiritual and financial support of my Congregational Leadership Team (past and present) and my Sisters (Sisters of Charity of the Incarnate Word of Houston). I am very thankful!

I am indebted to the professors and staff members of Aquinas Institute of Theology, St. Louis, MO, USA, for their magnanimous and generous contributions towards my academic growth. I thank my academic advisers, Sr. Colleen Mallon (who also wrote the foreword), Sr. Catherine Vincie, and Fr. José Santiago, for journeying with me and giving me challenging but positive feedback. I sincerely appreciate the support and kind advice of my professors: Fr. George Boudreau, Fr. Richard Peddicord (former President, Aquinas Institute), Carolyn Wright, Sr. Carla Mae Streeter, Fr. Seán Charles Martin, and Fr. Don Goergen.

My profound gratitude goes to my former bishop, Most Rev. Dr. Lucius Ugorji, for inspiring and supporting me.

My family members rendered their wonderful encouragement. I acknowledge the prayerful support and love of my mum, Daa Luu, my loving and late father, Dee Joe, and my beloved and cherished siblings, Fr. Udo, Gloria, Henry, and Prisca. I experience irreplaceable love from my niece Amarachi, my nephews Chigozie, Akachukwu, Enyioma, Gerald, Chimdike, and Gregory, and my Sister-in-law Nkiru. I love you all!

My friends greatly helped me. I am thankful to Dr. Austin Igbuku, Mr. Pius Ogiji, Sr. Elizabeth N. Okpalaenwe for writing the preface, and to Frs. Emmanuel Foro and Reginald Temu, thank you for your support.

My warm appreciation is also extended to CUEA Press Publishers, especially Rev. Dr. Patrick Tawale, for publishing this work for the first time, Paul Karanja and the Kolbe Press for printing it in 2015, and En Route Books and Media, especially Dr. Sebastian Mahfood, OP, for republishing it in 2024. You are all dear to me; thank you!

I honor those who shared their stories and allowed me to use them in this reflection. The list is endless; thus, I am grateful to all who supported me in one way or another throughout the writing of this book. May God reward and bless you!

Foreword

The reality of domestic violence and its destructive impact on families and individuals can never be overstated. Suffering the violence of those who seek to achieve power over another is always an experience of contrast that leaves the victim questioning his or her own self-worth. Sr. Adaku Ogbuji, in this book, seeks to address the conditions of domestic violence among African families and suggests specific actions that the ministry of the Church might take to stem the tide of violence, often hidden, among African families.

As a student at Aquinas Institute of Theology, St. Louis, Missouri, Sr. Adaku learned first-hand about the destructive consequences of domestic abuse. Moved by the stories of women whom she served in several safe houses, she began to question the reality of domestic abuse in her home country, Nigeria, and the socio-cultural conditions that keep women in situations of abuse. This became the topic of her MA thesis, which I had the privilege of advising, and this text is the fruit of her thesis.

Delving deeply into the work of Fr. Robert Schreiter, CPPS, Sr. Adaku introduces the reader to how violence functions in human relationships and the effective steps needed to assist victims in their healing journey. She also outlines the ways in which false understandings of the reconciliation process can short-circuit this journey. She offers examples from those who have graciously allowed her to share their stories in the hope that others might experience liberation from the evil of domestic violence.

Sr. Adaku also enjoins Church leaders to be active agents resisting the evil of domestic violence and supporting the conditions for true reconciliation.

Since graduating with dual degrees, Master of Theology and Master of Divinity from Aquinas Institute, Sr. Adaku has been serving in Kenya as the novice director for her religious community, the Sisters of Charity of the Incarnate Word, Houston. Her work in this text is a testimony of hope and compassion. Grounded in faith, she believes in the power of the Risen Christ to undo all the wrongs of violence inflicted on the innocent. The book seeks to be a concrete expression of God's love directed towards those most in need of healing from domestic violence.

Sr. Colleen Mary Mallon, O.P., Ph.D.
Aquinas Institute of Theology
Feast of St. Therese of the Little Flower
October 1, 2015

Preface

This book, *Dealing Effectively with Domestic Abuse: The ministry of Reconciliation and Healing*, highlights the question of reconciliation, healing, and forgiveness in human life in a very innovative way. Major concerns about women's situations in families, which are featured in the works of a number of preceding writers, are reiterated with a new voice. There are burning issues the writer of this book wants to bring to the readers' awareness. Sr. Helen Adaku Ogbuji, a Theologian, Spiritual Director, and Formator, has been working with women in different countries.

She wishes to bring into open the need to pay attention to the domestic problems and violence encountered by many women from African cultural contexts, especially in Nigeria and Kenya. Many are wounded and traumatized and, in their situation, they have no voice. They have been intimidated by culture and society. Their stories and the reasons for the abuse were very similar among the sampled women the writer pointed out in this work. She described their experiences as "the Evils of violence in families." She listened and brought their painful stories to prayer and to God. She also made practical suggestions that can lead one to reconcile with herself and then move towards forgiveness.

There are practical lessons the writer wants us to learn from this book. Violence does not pay. Both the victims and perpetrators suffer in the end. It robs everybody of the peace of mind which is inherent in us and replaces it with hatred, fear, and violence which does not come from God.

This book is appropriate for families who are finding it difficult to come out from their debased life of hatred, violence, and unforgiving hearts. It is for women who may not know or understand how to handle their domestic issues. It is for men who are trapped in their violent behavior against women, children, and their fellow men. It is for women who engage their fellow women in the evil of violence and expose them to prostitution. They may not know the value of human life and the dignity God has bestowed on us. This book is valid for formators, educators, and those who journey with the vulnerable people as it offers relevant perspectives for an approach to interpreting the domestic life situation in general and the steps to move towards healing and reconciliation. I recommend this book to everyone because we all come from families.

Sr. Dr. Elizabeth Ngozi Okpalaenwe, MSHR
Senior Lecturer, Department of Counselling Psychology
Catholic University of Eastern Africa, Kenya

Definition of Terms

Patriarchy: Patriarchal society in this work is defined as the social setting where men are the heads of the families, and thus women and children are under the authority of men. In a patriarchal society, some women suffer oppression and subordination as men exert influence over them. Women are to be seen and not to be heard; their abode is in the kitchen, and their main function is to procreate children, preferably male children. Most of the time, they are excluded from the leadership of the family, society, and the Church. Decision-making is not within their reach, and they are prohibited from officiating in most societal rituals.

Abuse: Any violent word, action, or behavior that is threatening or which inflicts pain on another physically, emotionally, spiritually, socially, or economically. In this work, abuse will be used interchangeably with violence.

Women: In this work, the term "women" is used generically to include older women, young girls, and female children.

Reconciliation: This work follows Robert Schreiter's definition of reconciliation. Reconciliation is what God does through the victim of abuse. It is the ability of the abused person to discover the divine grace within her and seek healing.

Healing: In this reflection, healing is the process of curing the wounds and restoring the physical, emotional, and spiritual wholeness of violence victims.

Forgiveness: Forgiveness is a state where the victim of abuse moves from having the experience of being battered control her life to a whole new life and stance that does not feel like bondage.

Introduction

"Husbands, love your wives, as Christ loved
the church and gave himself up for her."

- Eph. 5:25

"Forget the past and forgive him" is a passionate and fervent appeal that sometimes breaks the hearts of many wounded Christians who are hurting and finding it difficult to forgive. The wounded heart needs to be mended slowly and progressively. However, in the gradual process of trying to bring about healing and reconciliation, the reconcilers tend to hurry the process, sometimes making the victims believe they cannot forgive. This was the experience of the women with whom I journeyed during my Supervised Practice of Ministry in the U.S.A. at a transitional safe home for abused women and their children. These wounded women confessed that they longed to forgive their abusers, but they needed time to go through the process without feeling that they were rushed.

During this ministerial experience, the violence in families and what some women go through awakened in me the desire to study the experiences of women and the faces of different abuses that are rarely mentioned. As I ministered to these wounded women, my horizon was broadened concerning the trauma some women face at home because of domestic abuse. The trauma of abuse against women and the painful stories I listened to during this time accompanied me to prayer. Their stories and the reasons for the abuse were very similar among these women.

Below are two samples of the abuse cases that I handled. Both stories are told during our support group weekly meetings. Their names were changed to protect the victims, and the name of the Home for Abused was also not included. What I have illustrated here is the case study of one of the group members of twelve abused women from different cultures – Asia, America, Central America, and Africa – who lived in this safe house and how I helped them process their stories. We met weekly to share their painful stories. This sharing helped them to begin the process of healing and embracing a new life as dignified women. The second case followed the same process, but I will elaborate only on the first case study.

Case 1

Wino was abandoned by her mother in a Laundromat when she was six years old. She was taken to different foster homes, and in these homes, she was physically and sexually abused. As a young adolescent, she needed to love and to be loved. Thus, she "fell in love" with an older guy. This guy initially appeared to have loved and cared for her. For once, she felt loved. After about a year, the man became abusive. He abused her physically, emotionally, and sexually. Wino was ashamed even to tell anyone. She had no family or anyone to direct and reassure her that she could be helped and where to find help. Wino was wrestling and blaming herself as the cause of her problem, "If my mother could abandon me, then anyone can abandon me. I am not good enough."

Reflective Questions that Guided My Sharing with These Twelve Women:

- As you listen to this story, what feelings/memories stir up in you?
- What could be the heart of the matter of this case, or what could be the core concern or central theme of the case?
- From personal experience or culture, how have you seen this type of situation at work?
- What do you find helpful or unhelpful about the case and its process?

Summary of how the Story was Processed

After reading the case twice with the clarifying questions above, we started reflecting on the feelings. They mentioned anger, sadness, displeasure, bitterness, frustration, pain, disappointment, and helplessness, as well as joy and hope since the first victim was able to recognize that she was not good enough and may possibly work toward her self-esteem.

The heart of the matter was surrounded around learning to love oneself again, searching for authentic love and acceptance with whatever one calls a family or a support system, forgiveness, and letting go so that the past hurtful feelings of abandonment and rejection do not have control over an individual, as well as creating a safe avenue where losses are processed. Finally, the core question was: How can a person work on self-pity by learning to forgive, loving herself again, and extending that love to others? Is it possible to love again? If yes, how does one restore trust that was betrayed and the problem of insecurity that engulfs an abused person?

More than half of the women confessed that this case study apparently relates to their experiences. Some explained that their mother had died, and they were left in foster homes where they were abused. Others explained that they were abandoned by their parents with no support system to turn to. All the women admitted that they always thought they were not good enough until they started working on their self-esteem. They expressed their disappointment with the systems – religious, political, and social – that sometimes do not support women and children who face abuse at the hands of men.

Basically, most of the women admitted that hearing other women's stories helped them in their moments of grief. It gave them the courage to share their stories and realize they are not alone. In addition, some mentioned the importance of forgiveness, self-love, and acceptance, and many expressed that these virtues were helpful to them in their grieving and healing process. The process was also useful since it helped the women to reflect on their wounds as they compared their stories with the case study. Another helpful thing was the comment of one of the women to her fellow peers: "Life is too short; get over your grudges." I thought this was very insightful and a big lesson for the women.

Case 2

When Eve married in a Catholic tradition, her relationship with her husband was very intimate. After the birth of their first baby boy, the husband began to return home late, sometimes drunk, and sometimes she was beaten for no apparent reason. With time, the frequency of the physical, sexual, and economic abuses was alarming and was weaved together with affection when the man was sober. Her first trusted place to seek assistance was her parish priest, who advised her to return home and pray for her husband to repent. This client acknowledged that the abuse had become a daily activity even as she continued to pray. Her abuser threatened to divorce her if she made the abuse public. Eve is an immigrant in the USA without legal papers, and her husband is an American citizen. So, his divorcing her would consequently mean deportation. However, after being battered until miscarriage, Eve escaped one night from her home and found shelter in a Home for Abused Women. Among other things she suffered was the enduring physical, emotional, and spiritual pain from her husband. Eve kept asking herself: "Where did I go wrong? What can I do to make my marriage work? Am I the cause of this abuse, and am I to be blamed? I love my family, and I want my marriage to work, but I cannot take the abuse anymore."

The case study on Wino and Eve, as well as other stories that will be used in this narrative, compelled me to write on the reality of domestic abuse in Africa, which for so long and in too many cases has gone unnoticed, and how to raise awareness to the evils of this violence. It is good to mention that all the stories were used with the permission of those involved, and their names were changed to protect their privacy. This reflection will demonstrate that domestic violence in Africa is eating deeply into the fabric of family life. Many educated women prefer to remain single mothers rather than commit themselves to married life. Some see marriage as out of fashion and not ready to make that life-long commitment. Some women who are married are not enjoying their married lives because they are helplessly suffering at the hands of their spouses. Many women who are victims of abuse take antidepressants or sleeping pills to combat depression, mood swings, anger, and anxiety. Sometimes, when some women are diagnosed with mood disorders or depression because of sexual abuse, violence, and lack of family support, they are sometimes asked by their medical practitioners to take antidepressants.[1] I am wondering what solution the taking of these drugs can bring towards healing of violence. The drugs might give instant serenity and calmness and put someone to sleep, but the reality of the trauma of violence would remain unabated. The question to ask is, what alternatives to drug therapies are available?

Apart from taking drugs, some women run to witch doctors for love potions. Witch doctors are native doctors who use local herbs and incantations to cure those who are bewitched and those who seek solutions to their problems. Some married women (even unmarried ladies) seek their help when they need their husband's love and want to keep their spouses happily married to them without violence. Celestina Nwankwoala, a Nigerian woman, expresses: "The

---

[1] Diane Saibil, "SSRIAntidepressant: Their Place in Women's Lives" Women and Health Protection, www.whp-apsf.ca/en/documents/ssri.html.

sooner Nigerian women take the initiative and understand that they should be in control of their lives and solely responsible for their growth and success, the sooner the abuse of women will stop." She continues: "Women in this country have lost the confidence to move on and to exercise control and relevance in a relationship; some resort to giving their partners a love potion."[2] I am unsure how effective this love potion is, but stories abound that some men could become wild with hatred for their partner after being fed this concoction.

The Herald newspaper of Zimbabwe captured a piece of news of a woman whom her husband physically abused because the husband claimed that the wife, Mutsimu, gave him a love potion. The affidavit from the woman against the man states: "I am sick and tired of being physically abused by Lovemore. He comes to my mother's house where I am staying, assaulting me, saying I gave him a love potion. Whenever he starts physically abusing me, he will be shouting, saying he will kill me if I don't make him vomit the love potion I gave him."[3]

In Kenya, especially in urban areas, it is not difficult to find posters on electric poles advertising a mganga (a witch or traditional doctor) who gives medicine for a love potion, business prosperity, and cures many illnesses. In Ukambani, Kenya, a traditional medicine man interviewed by Catherine Wambua, a KTN (Kenya Television

---

[2] Celestina Nwankwoala, *A Letter to my Countrymen* (Bloomington, IN: Author House, 2013), 52.

[3] *The Herald,* November 24, 2014, "He Threatens to Kill Me, Woman Tells Court" (www.Herald.Co.Zw/he-threatens-to-kill-me-woman-tells-court.html).

Network) news reporter, boasted that "all kinds of women, including those who are materially endowed and live in Nairobi, seek love potions and pay handsomely for their services."[4]

Although some women's intention for a love potion is to save their marriage and not to harm their husbands, this might backfire, and the love will be transformed into hatred. Love is not something to acquire through magic. It is a gift from God. The solution to violence and peaceful coexistence is not to use magical concoctions to win a partner. Elechi Amadi, a Nigerian novelist, tells the story of how Ahurole used a love potion on her husband, Ekwueme. When this backfired, the husband became very violent and sick, and he finally landed in the hands of another woman, Ihuoma.[5]

The children are also affected by family conflicts and violence since they might be learning and possibly could practice the aggressive behaviors of their parents. Because these families make up the domestic, local, and universal church as well as part of the human community, the church and every person who values justice, peace, and harmony have the sacred obligation to work towards emancipating abused women from their misery and marital prison.

This book entitled *Dealing Effectively with Domestic Abuse: The Ministry of Reconciliation and Healing* – my little contribution to the cause of healing battered women – reflects on the different faces of abuse and how to help the wounded victims go through the process

---

[4] Art Matters. Info, "Love Charms in Modern Urban Homes," posted 28 September 2008, www.artmatters.Info/heritage-formerly-culture/2008/09/love-charms-in-modern-urban-homes.html

[5] Elechi Amadi, *The Concubine* (London: Heinemann Educational Books, 1966).

of authentic reconciliation in order to experience peace and healing. The question that I reflected on is: What can the Church communities do to facilitate the process of reconciliation and healing? The reconciliation theories by Robert Schreiter, which offer effective ecclesial responses to violence, will be used in this work to contribute to the dynamics that can help the abused women go through this reconciliation journey. Focusing on two African cultures (Nigeria and Kenya), this reflection will illustrate how an authentic reconciliation process may bring about healing to victims of abuse and, perhaps, the repentance of the abuser. Some recommendations will be presented that may aid in reducing violence against women in African society and hopefully in the global world.

I am aware that some men suffer abuse in the hands of women, especially in some parts of Kenya, Nigeria, and other African countries where men are physically beaten and battered by women. Through the *Capital News*, Catherine Karongo explained on the 16th of February, 2012, that 460,000 men were battered yearly in Central Kenya and the Nairobi area according to the statistics by Maendeleo Ya Wanaume (an organization in Kenya for the empowerment of men founded by Mr. Nderitu Njoka) which was a higher figure from the 160,000 men recorded in 2009.[6] Although this figure could be exaggerated, some people in Kenya blamed the government for taking too much interest in empowering women at the expense of men. Sometimes, women who are strong enough in nature and are wronged by way of infidelity, drug or alcohol addiction, and financial

---

[6] Rachel Muthoni, "Kenya: Poverty, Alcoholism Blamed for Rising Domestic Violence Against Men," *The WIP* (June 13, 2012).

and emotional neglect by their partners take to violence. Rachel Muthoni, quoting Mary Wamaitha, writes, "He comes home drunk every day. He does not contribute to the needs of the children and does not fulfill my conjugal rights. Why not discipline him?" Rachel continues that some men drink the cheap illicit brew from morning till night without doing any job. Thus, women are left to fend for the family through their daily casual and meager jobs.[7]

Recently, on the 5th and 6th of June 2015, respectively, two women from Central Kenya chopped off the private parts of their spouses in an episode of domestic violence because of marital infidelity and drunkenness. *The Citizen Television* reported that the forty-year-old man allegedly stayed out late drinking and returned home drunk. Upon discovering condoms in his pocket, the man's wife decided he no longer needed his external reproductive organs and severed them. The second incident, which occurred on the 9th of June, 2015, was that the man had returned home drunk, and after an argument over money, the wife stabbed him twice on the genital part. This was so challenging for most men that one businessman, Barre Apiyo, invented the genitalia shield.[8]

It is also possible that some women who are gainfully employed or more educated than their partners may treat their husbands with disdain and contempt. Some wives can become unfaithful to their spouses and deny them conjugal rights because there is another man outside their matrimonial home. However, these incidences are only

---

[7] Catherine Karongo, "400,000 Kenyan Men Battered Yearly," *CFM News*, 16th February 2012.

[8] Jambonewspot.Com, Posted Wednesday, June 17, 2015.

a handful compared to what women go through in our society today. We are not advocating for violence against any gender. However, this book is seeking for an alternative way to seek reconciliation when violence occurs, as well as the principle of love – The Golden Rule – "Treat others as you would love to be treated" (Romans 12:17; Matthew 5: 38-40).

This golden rule reminds me of a story of a foolish man who, upon learning that the Buddha observed the principle of great love, which commends the return of good for evil, decided to abuse him. The Buddha asked him, "Son, if one declined to accept a present made to him, to whom would it belong?" The foolish man answered, "In that case, it would belong to the one who offered it." "My son," said the Buddha, "you have railed at me, but I decline to accept your abuse, and I request you to keep it to yourself. As the echo belongs to the sound, and the shadow to its substance, so does your misery belong to you."[9] In the same way, this book seeks to encourage the victims of violence to reject and refuse the gift given to them in the form of abuse.

In this work, I focused only on women because the cultural paradigm is patriarchal, which mainly works in men's favor, and the women are, therefore, left in a vulnerable state. Also, a man's physical strength gives him more advantage, and statistics show that many men engage in abusive retribution as a way to resolve marital matters. No one deserves to be abused, and there are better ways to settle issues that arise from marital relationships. This reflection aims to

---

[9] Deepak Gupte, Wisdom 101: The Best Gift you Can Give Yourself (Bloomington, IN: Xlibris Corporation, 2009), 11.

initiate a conversation that fosters respect, reconciliation, fairness, and peace among married couples experiencing disagreements. This approach, as it addresses the issue of domestic violence and the healing of battered women, also hopes to resolve men's legitimate concerns that sometimes lead to abuse.

There are five chapters in this book; chapter one will analyze the meaning of domestic abuse, the different kinds of abuse, the effects of violence on children, and the conditions that could make domestic violence possible. Through the documents of the Church, chapter two will elucidate the dignity of women. Chapter three will explain, through the work of Robert Schreiter, what reconciliation is and illustrate the relationship between reconciliation and violence. It will clarify how violence distorts the true story of an individual, the different models of reconciliation, and the genuine reconciliation process. Chapter four will explain what healing is and how the victims of abuse may experience healing through the journey of reconciliation. It will also shed light on what forgiveness does in the healing process, the role of the Church in the healing process, the role of the support group in the healing process, and the power of ritual in the healing process. Finally, chapter five will give some recommendations that can help to abate the rate at which domestic violence is increasing in our society.

It is my hope that this reflection will help pastors and priests of different denominations, catechists of different parishes, lay faithful leaders, small Christian communities, religious men and women who accept candidates from these broken homes, and wounded women and men who are seeking answers to how to redeem the dignity of women who have been abused in their homes and societies.

Families form the branches of the domestic church, the foundation of faith in God, and the first school where love is taught and practiced. However, when families turn out to be the most brutal and hostile unit in society, then the Mother Church and humanity will be affected adversely. A healthy family, therefore, makes for a healthy Church and society! Although this book is written in the context of domestic abuse and ways to attain the grace of healing through reconciliation, it can be helpful in many other life situations where reconciliation is needed, for instance, during religious community tussles or when friends are in conflict, or when we are finding solution and healing after societal wars, etc.

Chapter 1

The Meaning of Domestic Violence with the Experiences of African Women

> "Don't use foul or abusive language. Let everything you say be good and helpful, so that your words will be an encouragement to those who hear them."
>
> - Ephesians 4:29

"He doesn't believe I have any rights of my own. If I say no, he beats me. That is not what I want in life."[1] This is the voice of Mrs. Isimeto-Osibuamhe, a Nigerian wife who shared her story of how her husband mistreated her. Since her wedding in 1997, she has been beaten more than 60 times. And some of these abuses took place while she was pregnant. He once threw a lantern at her and, on another occasion, held a knife to her throat while a friend pleaded with him not to kill her. Mrs. Isimeto-Osibuamhe explained that when she went to the police, they told her that she was a grown woman, and she could get a divorce if she did not want to be married. They were dismissive of her plight and perhaps were indicating that being beaten is part of marriage, which she ought to take if she wanted to stay married. When she told her father-in-law about the abuse, he declared to her that "beating is normal." When she told her local

---

[1] Sharon Lafraniere, "Entrenched Epidemic: Wife Beatings in Africa," *New York Times*, August 11, 2005.

priest, he advised her that her husband was the head of the household and she should be submissive to him. He encouraged her to avoid making him angry and submit to his decisions. The priest appeared to suggest that Mrs. Isimeto-Osibuamhe should have accepted her husband's choices and decisions, even when they were misguided.

On September 10th, 2011, the Nigerian newspaper *The Guardian* reported how women took to the streets of Lagos on a "Walk Against Domestic Violence."[2] This walk was organized in honor of a thirty-year-old mother, Titilayo Ariwoyo, who was beaten to death by her husband. The protesting women called on all women to desist from hiding the shame of domestic violence, but rather to expose the abuser.

Florence Wanjiku, a Kenyan woman, lived in an abusive relationship for ten years. According to her: "My husband came home drunk one night. He went to the kitchen, grabbed the wooden spoon, and started beating me up the way you will beat a little child, using a stick. But unfortunately, he hit me so hard that it broke on my scalp and my scalp got a cut. It was so deep that I had to be stitched with eight stitches around there."[3]

On the 2nd of July 2013, the *Kenyan Daily Nation* carried the news of the experience of sexual abuse and rape of a young girl. The girl, whose name was not disclosed, lamented: "I woke up to find a

---

[2] Ebere Ameh, "A Walk Against Domestic Violence," *The Guardian* (September 10, 2011): 1.

[3] Majtenyi Report, "Cases of Domestic Violence Increase in Kenya," *Voice of America*, March 4, 2010, www.voanews. Com/content/cases-of-domestic-violence-increase-in-ke-gust 11, 2005.

man on top of me, his friend waiting for his turn."[4] This story explains how this young girl was drugged and raped by several men and finally dumped along the wayside. The four instances above may be the fate of many married and unmarried women in Africa or even in our world today; however, only a few women were bold enough to tell their stories.

Domestic abuse is any hurtful word or behavior from a spouse against his/her partner or children that is intentionally threatening and/or inflicts pain. Abuse in marriage manifests in various forms: physical, emotional, verbal, psychological, spiritual, social, and economic. Domestic abuse leads to violence and injuries, oppression, depression, tearful and sorrowful living, dysfunctional and broken marriages, and has physical, psychological, financial, and developmental effects on children. In extreme cases, it can result in the death of one or both parties involved.

Throughout history, women have frequently been mistreated in male-dominated societies. The phrase "rule of thumb" originated in Medieval England, where a man was allowed to beat his wife with a stick as long as it wasn't wider than his thumb.[5] Patriarchal society is a social setting where men are the heads of the families; thus, women and children are under the authority of men. This social setting is not bad in itself, but it can become oppressive when the power

---

[4] Peter Oduor, "A Drink, a Pill, and Lots of Tears: Inside Kenya's Silent Epidemic of Drugging, Raping, and Dumping," *Daily Kenya Living* 2, *Daily Nation* (July 2, 2013): 2-3.

[5] James N Poling, "Male Violence Against Women and Children," in *The Care of Men*, eds. Christie C. Neuger and James N. Poling (Nashville, TN: Abingdon Press, 1997), 150.

invested in men by the patriarchal society is misused. When this power is misused, women are sometimes seen as inferior to men, and their status varies from being helpers to being regarded as property owned by men. Some men have supported this culture by quoting various scriptural passages; e.g., the creation of Eve from the rib of Adam (Genesis 2:22), and St. Paul's admonishment that women should be submissive to men (Ephesians 5:22-24). Many women have faced exploitation in the form of denial of inheriting assets from families or properties, economic marginalization, female circumcision, lack of formal education, wife battering, horrible widowhood practices, sexual abuse, and rape.

Many women also live in fear of disclosing the abuse because of so many threats. Although shrouded in silence, domestic abuse is real and continues to crush many African women. In their study of violence against women in Nigeria, professors of sociology at the University of Ibadan, Nigeria – Kolawole Oyediran and Uche Isiugo-Abanihe – noted that the Nigerian society is so supportive of man's superiority that even if there is evidence of physical assault and injury on the woman, the society will blame the woman for whatever that has happened to her.[6] According to their sociological research, some women even see abuse as a sign of love and as a disciplinary measure to keep women and children in check.

Domestic violence may begin with flimsy justifications, such as bad cooking, giving birth only to girls/barrenness, disrespecting the

---

[6] Kolawole Oyediran and Uche Isiugo-Abanihe, "Perceptions of Nigerian Women on Domestic Violence: Evidence from 2003 Nigeria Demographic and Health Survey," *African Journal of Reproductive Health* 9, no. 2 (August 2005): 39.

in-laws, or leaving the house without the permission of the husband. The frequency of this violence is very alarming, and at the same time, it is condoned, invisible, and underreported. When physical abuse by the husband occurs, it is shrouded in silence. Sometimes, extended families hesitate to intervene, calling the abuse "a family problem that requires a family solution." Often, the wife is abused when the man is intoxicated, when his food is served late, when he is envious, when he is under the influence of drugs, when he is unemployed, or when his boss frustrates him at the office. Some men believe that physical discipline is culturally accepted and that it is the husband's right. Sometimes, they even blame the woman for their violent reaction. The United States Catholic bishops captured the issue very well when they wrote: "Typically, abusive men deny that the abuse is happening, or they minimize it. They often blame their abusive tendencies on someone or something other than themselves. They tell their partner, 'You made me do this.'"[7]

The Eastern and Central Africa Women in Development Network discovers that 90% of cases of violence against women and girls happen in the family.[8] Quoting the daily intake of new cases of domestic violence by the International Federation of Women Lawyers-Kenya, Angellina Mwau explains that about 5200 Kenyan women experience domestic abuse every year. Similarly, the cases of some

---

[7] United States Conference of Catholic Bishops, "When I Call for Help: A Pastoral Response to Domestic Violence Against Women," November 12, 2002. http://www.usccb.org/laity/help.shtml.

[8] Eastern and Central African Women in Development Network, "Violence Against Women: Trainers' Manual" (Nairobi, Kenya: Paulines Publications Africa, 2011), 29.

homicides that are reported in *Kenyan Daily Nation Newspaper* are usually related to domestic violence.[9] In his research, Aihie Ose, a Nigerian counselor, notes that in 2007, Amnesty International reported that two-thirds of Nigerian women had been subjected to physical, psychological, sexual, and emotional abuse by either their husbands, partners, or fathers. Ose reports that 70% of the respondents have been abused in their families, with 92% of the victims being female. The common forms of this domestic abuse include shouting 93%, slapping and pushing 77%, and punching and kicking 40%.[10] However, the culture of silence concerning violence against women is so overwhelming that finding any relevant statistics is sometimes difficult. It is very troubling that many women do not report abuse. Their reasons include: shame, fear of being divorced, cultural influence, the belief that divorce is a taboo, fear of the threats of the abuser, fear for the safety of the children, worry about the continuity of marriage, and the belief that marriage is for life, economic reasons, and pressure from the society and the Church. The ugliest part of this scenario is that even when the abuse is reported to civil society, the police force sometimes dismisses complaints of domestic violence as a private or family matter.[11]

---

[9] Angellina Mwau, "Counseling Victims of Domestic Violence in Kenya," in *African Women's Health*, ed. Meredeth Turshen (Asmara, Eritrea: Africa World Press, 2000), 107.

[10] Aihie Ose, "Prevalence of Domestic Violence in Nigeria: Implications for Counseling," *Edo Journal of Counseling* 2, no. 1 (May 2009): 2-3.

[11] Ose, 2-3. See also Angelina Mwau, *Counseling Victims of Domestic Violence in Kenya*, 108.

Chapter 1: The Meaning of Domestic Violence 21

Unfortunately, some women who are victims of domestic violence do not receive help from society. Thus, they adapt to these unfortunate practices as customary and even as an acceptable way of life. According to the research conducted by Ose, "64.4% of married women and 50.4% of unmarried women in Nigeria expressed consent to wife beating."[12] Because some victims of violence have accepted their fate and see themselves as "no good," they regard violent behavior as normal or a sign of love. In many instances, victims of abuse are not listened to or considered innocent, so they suffer from self-blame. Thus, some women endure their agony in silence and face ridicule from their spouses, who sometimes rationalize or downplay the abuse and even blame the victims for provoking them. Repeated ridicule relegates women to the background so that they uncon-

---

[12] Ibid.

sciously accept their fate, especially when they are not supported by society or by their family members.

Angellina Mwau, a Kenyan counselor, points out that in some Kenyan societies, the victims of domestic abuse are often blamed rather than the abuser. She clarifies that even when a woman is seriously injured, her family may encourage her to return home and fulfill her role as a good wife.[13] Certainly, being a good woman omits condoning, ignoring, disregarding, or tolerating the cruelty of a partner. It would be wonderful if husbands received the best from their wives, including respect, good companionship, honesty, fidelity, love, trust, good communication, a pleasant personality, a supportive spirit, dedication, appreciation, loyalty, a clean appearance, a decorated home, and other sacrifices or help that keep married couples together. However, the question remains: are husbands ready to offer their spouses the same standards and values they expect from them? Or are these demands only expected from women? In other words, is the ball only in the woman's court to play? Some individuals daydream about the perfect partner, spouse, in-laws, kids, and house. However, in reality, there is no perfect human being. This reminds me of the popular anecdote about a man who traveled everywhere looking for the perfect wife. He almost found one, but the woman he wanted to marry was also seeking the perfect husband. I think it is time to wake up and embrace the beauty of the reality of our imperfection, whatever it has to offer, and say "no" to domestic violence and "yes" to peaceful coexistence instead of accepting fate as victims of abuse or perpetuating violence as abusers. When married couples

---

[13] Mwau, 108.

have an open mind about each other's flaws and show tolerance while respectfully helping themselves to grow, they perfect their union, and its longevity is guaranteed.

As I reflect on how the victims of domestic violence become vulnerable and resign to their fate, I also tend to think about the experience of some women who stood their ground to fight for their right to human dignity. In doing so, they gained the respect and love of their husbands. This observation is congruent with the saying that men admire, esteem, love, and respect strong-headed women who have opinions of their own and who stand up for what they believe is right. Could the right to the human dignity of abused women be restored if they stand up for their rights and refrain from resigning to the fate of accepting the brutality and harsh treatment by some men?

No woman deserves to be treated without respect, either by her husband, partner, friend, or fiancé. The act of correction, reproach, admonition, rebuke, and reprimand can be done with love, compassion, and all gentleness without being vicious or violent. A pastoral theologian, Rita-Lou Clarke agrees that no one deserves to be beaten. Although a woman may appear to provoke, she may be unpleasant, a bitch, and act badly, but she is still not responsible for the abuser's act of violence.[14]

The abuser is certainly responsible for his act of brutality, and he is not justified if he is cruel to his wife or children. However, what is experienced sometimes is that women are blamed for an act of

---

[14] Rita-Lou Clarke, *Pastoral Care of Battered Women* (Philadelphia, PA: The Westminster Press, 1986), 17.

violence by the man. She is accused of nagging, rudeness, not keeping the house in order, not caring for the children properly, being a bad cook, etc. This is not to say that men are not recipients of abuse or that women should not make changes in their behavior, especially those who exhibit unbecoming behavior. The fact is that no adult is responsible for another adult's unconscionable action or reaction. We can ask: What makes an adult culpable or morally responsible for his/her actions? The adult who performs it must have knowledge of it, or he did it intentionally. Secondly, the adult is free to choose whether or not to carry it out. And, finally, he has the will to see it through. These personal functions are not transferable from one person to another. Therefore, the partner of an abusive man is not responsible for his violent behavior.

Different Faces of Abuse

Physical Abuse

"A man who appeals to violence and intimidation is ignorant of the power of reason and persuasion." This is an African proverb that condemns bullying, but encourages the use of common sense and reasonable dialogue in settling disputes. The use of physical force, such as kicking, slapping, punching, hair-pulling, stabbing, choking, pushing, beating, and biting, to inflict harm is not acceptable. Physical abuse is worldwide and cuts across income, class, and culture. Chinua Achebe, a Nigerian novelist, captures family life among the Igbos of Nigeria and presents how Okonkwo, the novel's hero, ruled his household with a heavy hand. He was said to have beaten his wife

Ojiugo on the flimsy reason that Ojiugo went for a hair-do and did not return home on time to prepare Okonkwo's meal.[15]

Wife battering might cause death and serious physical injury and instill fear in the woman and in her children. A good example is the Kenyan *Daily Nation*, which reported thirteen cases of death through domestic violence within three months.[16] The same Kenyan *Daily Nation,* on October 5th, 2015, reported the news of a man from Tharaka-Nthi in Kenya, Isaac Mwasia, who stabbed his wife, a nurse, Alice Kathambi, several times. She sustained serious injuries on the head and was in critical condition. Thinking that the wife had died, Mr. Mwasia swallowed some poison and died. It was their son who alerted a neighbor who saved Mrs. Alice's life. And this neighbor confirmed that the stabbing could have been a result of a domestic dispute.[17]

The same *Daily Nation,* a couple of days after the above incident – October 7th, 2015 – recounted another sad story of a ninety-year-old man (from Embu, Kenya) who viciously slashed severally his wife, an eighty-seven-year-old grandmother, with a machete. Thinking he had killed his wife, he reported himself to the police and told them that "he had just killed someone." According to him, "his wife (Ms. Patricia Njeri) had been nagging him for so long, and he was fed up with her constant irritations." When the police arrived at the

---

[15] Chinua Achebe, *Things Fall Apart* (New York, NY: Alfred Knopf, Inc., 1992), 10, 24-25.

[16] Mwau, 107.

[17] Alex Njeru, "Man Commits Suicide after Stabbing Wife," *Daily Nation*, Nairobi, October 5th, 2015, p. 21.

crime scene, they found Ms. Njeri lying unconscious in a pool of her blood with multiple deep cuts on her head and limbs.[18]

Physical abuse in action

Wife battering is very common all over Africa, and women are mostly the victims. Two Nigerian Catholic priests, Des-Obi Obioma and Boniface Ogbenna, opined that physical abuse against women has one thing in common: they all originated from considering women as men's property through the payment of the bride price and as rooted in patriarchal society. (Bride price, dowry, or bride-wealth are gifts in the form of livestock or money that the family of a man gives in thanksgiving to the bride's family). This cultural practice is valued in all African countries, and it is not bad in itself. It is a sign of appreciation to the bride's family for bringing up their daughter

---

[18] Nation Correspondent, "Shock as Man, 90, Slashes 'Nagging' Wife," *Daily Nation*, October 7th, 2015, p. 11.

morally and uprightly. These writers explained that because patriarchal society operates on the assumption that women are created for men (or from men, as in the Book of Genesis), it gives some men a false sense of superiority. This archaic way of thinking consequently leads to many women being subjected to physical violence, discrimination, domination, and an unequal relationship.[19] The frequent experience of wife battering places a woman in a state of helplessness. Quoting Lenore Walker, Clarke explains, "The very fact of being a married woman automatically creates a situation of powerlessness."[20] After marriage, the powerless wife is under the man's control and authority. Sometimes, she suffers in silence and endures her husband's physical domination and violence.

Emotional and Psychological Abuse

Emotional abuse could be in the form of negative criticism, social isolation, intimidation, name-calling, shaming, or harming a woman's self-worth in order to put her down.[21] In many African cultures, abusive language has become an avenue to keep women in check and to relegate them to inferior positions in society. Some men threaten, scold, and drill fear into their wives. Their actions are often

---

[19] Des-Obi Obioma and Boniface Ogbenna, "Women Issues: Violence Against Women in Africa: An Exposition," in *The Kpim of Feminism: Issues and Women in a Changing World*, ed. George U Ukagba, Des-obi Obioma, and Iks Nwankwor (Victoria BC, Canada: Trafford, 2010), 330-331, 337.

[20] Clarke, 39. Quoted from: Lenore Walker, The Battered Woman (Harper and Row, 1979), 57.

[21] Ose, 4.

examples of emotional abuse with the use of demeaning and ill-advised remarks that make women feel like "second-class" citizens.[22] This abuse hurts the self-image of the victim. A man will remind a woman of how he paid her dowry; thus, he is the master of the household. The same derogatory message is sometimes aimed at unmarried young girls, pressuring them to believe that they have an expiration date unless they marry quickly. It is drummed into their heads that time waits for no one and their beauty can fade away when no man admires or wants to marry them. The saddest thing is that a good number of them may also be emotionally abused by their peers, especially young married women who boast of having their "own husbands."

Furthermore, most women struggling with infertility receive humiliating verbal attacks from some men; sometimes, they are addressed in a derogatory way, namely: "a man" or an "unfruitful tree." Akachi Ezeigbo, a Nigerian writer, explains this situation in her novel *The Last of the Strong Ones*, when Chieme's husband, Iwuchukwu, rejects her, saying, "I do not want to continue living with a person whom I cannot say is a male or a female."[23] In most African families, a marriage that is not blessed with children is considered fruitless and unfulfilling and may end up in a divorce. Quoting Buchi Emecheta, Benedict Nwachukwu-Udaku, a moral theologian, narrated how "a young Igbo woman, Nne Ego, was expelled from her

---

[22] Obioma and Ogbenna, 331.

[23] Akachi T. Ezeigbo, *The Last of the Strong Ones* (Lagos, Nigeria: Vista Books, 1998), 78.

marital home because she could not bear children."[24] Emotional abuse in form of insulting words stings and brings women of all classes to a state of helplessness, low self-esteem, inability to trust others, depression, as well as emotional pain.

Social-Cultural/Political Abuse

Politically, women in most African countries are meant to be seen and not to be heard. Although this is changing in this 21st century with many women becoming interested in politics, yet at the traditional/local level, women are not always allowed to participate in serious decision-making in the community. During most community decision-making sessions, women are not consulted because they are seen as inferior. Rose Uchem, a Catholic religious sister, explains that excluding women from "decision-making denies women voice in matters which ultimately bind them to the society. Men and women often have different perspectives on issues; thus, a decision made without women lacks the feminine dimension."[25] Could it be that men are sometimes afraid that women would come up with better ideas than them? In some cultures, when a woman wants to express her opinion in a community decision, she must first communi-

---

[24] Benedict Nwachukwu-Udaku, *From What We Should Do To Who We Should Be: Negotiating Theological Reflections and Praxis in the Context of HIV/AIDS Among the Igbos of Nigeria* (Bloomington, IN: Author House, 2011), 115.

[25] Rose Uchem, *Overcoming Women's Subordination in the Igbo African Culture and in the Catholic Church: Envisioning an Inclusive Theology with Reference to Women* (Enugu, Nigeria: Snaap Press, 2001), 17, 106.

cate it privately to her husband, who then conveys it to the entire community. In some Igbo communities in Nigeria, when a woman is outspoken in a community gathering, she is often subjected to derogatory name-calling like: "nwoke-nwanyi," or "oke-nwanyi" which means a woman who acts like a man.[26] This insidious statement aims to silence the victim and intimidate other women in social gatherings.

In some African cultures, there are some customs that are offensive to the body of a woman. They include: the female genital mutilation (FGM), forced widow inheritance, child marriage, and forced marriage. All these crimes are perpetrated against women without regard to their safety, respect for the way God created them, or the emotional damage these crimes might cause to their sexual lives. It is appalling that some cultures do not see anything wrong with these atrocities.

Let us have a look at the FGM, for instance: What is the advantage of partially removing the external genitalia of a girl? In some African communities, it is believed that FGM is necessary to reduce a girl's libido or sexual desire and to discourage her from sexual activities before marriage. In some cultures, FGM serves as an initiation into adulthood, i.e., the girl is ready for marriage. Are these reasons appropriate? What about the adverse effects of FGM, like bleeding to death, urinary infections, infertility, complications during childbirth, as well as the need for a reversal surgery when the victim faces many complications in life? FGM has no medical advantage, but it could rather cause more harm than good.

---

[26] Uchem, 87.

Chapter 1: The Meaning of Domestic Violence 31

The Voice of Victims of Abuse

During President Barack Obama's visit to Kenya (24th-26th July 2015), he addressed over 4500 Kenyans at Kasarani Stadium in Nairobi on the 26th of July 2015, and some of his speeches were on women's rights. He said:

> Around the world, there is a tradition of oppressing women and treating them differently and not giving them the same opportunities, and husbands beating their wives and children not being sent to school. Those are traditions. Treating women and girls as second-class citizens. Those are bad traditions. They need to change. They are holding you back. There's no excuse for sexual assault or domestic violence; there's no reason that young girls should suffer genital mutilation, and there's no place in a civilized society for the early or forced marriage of children. These traditions may go back centuries; they have no place in the 21st century. They are issues of right or wrong in any culture. But they are also

issues of success and failure. Any nation that fails to educate its girls or employ its women and allow them to maximize their potential is doomed to fall behind the global economy. We're in a sports center: imagine if you have a team and don't let half of the team play. That's stupid. That makes no sense.[27]

Certainly, some cultures or traditions do not make sense, but they are still kept. These include cultures that demand women kneel and serve their husbands' food or drink, where women are not permitted to eat until their husbands have eaten, and where it is perceived as a taboo for women to eat certain parts of an animal, like the gizzard of a chicken or the tongue of a cow.

Other cultures prohibit women from owning land and deny them property rights. Only male children in a family are considered lawful owners of their father's property. Thus, when an adult girl chooses a single lifestyle, she has no right to her father's property. Gladly, the amended Kenyan law has abolished this injustice, and a woman has the right to own property as well as to inherit and share in her father's property.

Another way that women face unjust treatment in society is when they are prohibited from performing some cultural rituals. In Nigeria, one such ritual is the kola-nut ritual – ịgọ ọjị. The kola nut ritual is the prayer for thanksgiving, peace, blessing, protection, and goodwill that unites the living and the dead. The kola nut (Ọjị Igbo) grows in the pod on the trees of cola acuminata, and the Igbos use it

---

[27] KTN News, Kenya, 26th July, 2015.

as a symbol of hospitality, peace, friendship, and unity.[28] Ọjị Igbo is very significant and symbolic in Igbo culture to the extent that the Igbos would say, "Onye wetara ọjị, wetara ndụ," meaning, that whoever brings the kola nut, brings life. This ritual involves blessing, breaking, sharing, and eating in table fellowship among community members, similar to the pattern of the Eucharistic ritual.

Uchem envisions that perhaps Jesus would have used a kola nut during the institution of the Holy Eucharist if he had been born an Igbo man.[29] Oji is given to a visitor as a sign of welcome and goodwill and used during public functions to offer prayer for the event's success and for the blessing of the people who gather for the event. People who are not on good terms do not share ọjị until they have reconciled. The eldest man in every gathering performs this ritual, and women are not to participate or be presented with the kola nut (Izi Oji). However, women can eat the nuts after they have been presented, blessed, broken, and shared by a man. During a gathering of only women, they may bless, break, and share the nuts privately. But when a man is present at the home or within the vicinity where the women are gathered, he will be asked to break the kola nut for them. The assumption is that women are inferior and not part of full members of society, which can be compared to the exclusion of women and children during the population census of the feeding miracles of the Gospels.

This culturally accepted tradition is also practiced during Christian gatherings. When this ritual is performed in a Christian setting,

---

[28] Uchem, 60.
[29] Uchem, 61.

women are reminded, "Anaghi ezi nwanyi ojị," which means that women are neither presented with the kola nut nor do they say the prayer of goodwill required by this sacred ceremony. However, women are to preserve the nut and make it available to their husbands for the rite. Uchem notes that this beautiful kola nut ritual, which is meant to celebrate inclusion, has become a symbol of domination and oppression of women both in society and in the church.[30] Certainly, it is male supremacy and cultural violence that continue to determine and dictate what a woman can or cannot do. The challenging question to ponder is: Is this cultural belief (that women should not perform the kola nut ritual in the social gathering of men and women) justifiable?

Sexual Abuse

Sexual violence is in the form of incest, forced sexual acts, rape, marital rape, sexual assault/harassment, using a girl for material gain or for prostitution, and child sexual abuse. Although men are most of the time accused of sexually abusing women, some women also make their money through having a brothel where girls are employed for prostitution. Sr. Elizabeth Okpalaenwe, a psychologist, portrays this picture well in her book *The Power to Succeed*. She explains how Mercy, the heroine of the novel, was brought from her village to the city with the intention of going to school, only to be

---

[30] Uchem, 60.

Chapter 1: The Meaning of Domestic Violence

forced into prostitution with other ladies. However, she escaped from that brothel to pursue her dream of being educated.[31]

In African society, sexual activity is sacred, and it is not discussed openly because sexual union involves the procreation of a new life. A woman or man who discusses sexual issues openly is often seen as a wayward or imprudent person. Quoting Izu Marcel Onyeocha, Nwachukwu-Udaku states that "sex was not a subject to be discussed glibly. It was considered remiss for adults to discuss matters regarding sexuality, and it was unthinkable for young people to make references to sexual issues before their elders."[32] Because sexual life is not a subject for discussion, it is hardly reflected in a joke, proverbs, or riddles, which are means of education among the Igbos of Nigeria. The secrecy about sex-talk forces young girls to learn about their sexual life from their aunts, sometimes from their mothers, older sisters, and mostly from their age groups or schoolmates.

Among the Igbos, chastity is a virtue only for women, and the sexual moral code forbids a girl from having sexual relations until she gets married.[33] Because of the fear of rejection that is associated with pregnancy outside of wedlock, a mother guides her daughters to cultivate the virtue of chastity, while little or nothing is said about their male counterparts. When a young girl moves into her husband's

---

[31] Elizabeth N. Okpalaenwe, *The Power to Succeed* (Menji, Cameroon: ANUCAM, 2005), 20-27.

[32] Nwachukwu-Udaku, 120-121.

[33] Michael Okoh, *Fostering Christian Faith in Schools and Christian Communities through Igbo Traditional Values: Towards a Holistic Approach to Christian Religious Education and Catechesis in Igboland* (Berlin, Germany: Lit VerLag, 2012), 57.

house as a virgin, her virginity not only brings honor and prestige to her but also to her parents, who are said to have trained her well. But when an unmarried girl becomes pregnant out of wedlock, she is ridiculed, and her pregnancy is referred to as imeokwa or imemkpuke i.e., inappropriate pregnancy, which are humiliating terms. The fruit of such a relationship is sometimes not accepted in families when the child is born, and the child does not share in the family assets.

Similarly, in Kenya, even as chastity is one-sided (girls are expected to be virgins), there is another demand from society to prove fertility, and that is premarital pregnancy becoming a prerequisite for marriage.[34] This attitude is a result of the sexually transmitted diseases which can cause infertility among couples. However, in recent years, pregnancy outside of marriage is not so much frowned upon in Kenyan society. Most women who find themselves in an unintended or intended pregnancy are happy to raise their children as single mothers without depending on the father of the child. Actually, the single parenthood is increasing all over the world because of the rise in divorce rate and the unwillingness of some women to live in an abusive relationship. However, the adverse effects of this single parenthood in children are enormous, even though it is becoming culturally accepted.

As virginity is stressed among girls, sometimes nothing is said about the chastity of men. A young man can impregnate a girl, and he refuses to take responsibility for the pregnancy. Sometimes, a

---

[34] Muthoni A. Mathai, *Sexual Decision-making and AIDS in Africa: A Look at the Social Vulnerability of Women in Sub-Saharan Africa to HIV/AIDS: A Kenyan Example* (Kassel, Ger- many: Kassel University Press, 2006), 255.

married man can have many mistresses, and the wife is not to complain. Benedict Nwachukwu-Udaku, a Nigerian moral theologian, explained that "a good woman is one who remains silent in the face of the disordered sexual life of her husband. Even as the husband is cheating on her, a good wife is expected to be loyal always to her husband when sexual demands are made."[35] Sometimes bosses in offices and teachers in schools demand sexual favors from their co-workers and students respectively. The victims are to remain silent about the abuse and never to complain if they need their jobs and if they want to "succeed academically."

Thus, sexual abuse is rarely reported in African culture. The report from the World Organization Against Torture in 2009 illustrates that after the post-election violence in Kenya in 2007/2008, many women and girls bore the worst violence through sexual abuse, especially among the internally displaced persons in the camps. This sexual abuse frequently occurs in Kenya, the report continues, but it is under-reported and treated as a private affair, especially marital rape. The law enforcement agents sometimes ridicule women who are bold enough to report the case.[36] This culture of silence is also portrayed when an uncle, a neighbor, a father, a brother, or a stranger rapes a girl and threatens her into silence. The *Daily Nation*, Nairobi, carried a sad story of young Alice, who was raped in 2013 by a neighbor at the age of eight years old. The rapist threatened both her and the younger brother, Brian (a five-year-old), with a gun, saying that

---

[35] Nwachukwu-Udaku, 118.

[36] Francesca Restifo et al., *Violence Against Women and Children in Kenya: An Alternative Report to the Committee Against Torture* (Geneva, Switzerland: World Organization Against Torture, 2009), 9.

he would kill them if they mentioned a word to anyone. Fortunately, he was later apprehended and charged in Nairobi court.[37]

The promotion of the culture of silence attests to the reason why sexual abuse is surrounded by secrecy. A woman remains silent when a man seeks to have a male child outside of his marital union because his wife has only female children or because she is struggling with infertility. This infidelity is never frowned upon or questioned in most African cultures. The culture of silence concerning issues of sexual life undermines the identity and the autonomy of a woman. Nwachukwu-Udaku expresses that any woman who openly challenges her husband's disordered sexual life in Igbo land is ridiculed by men as nwanyi wara anya, i.e., an imprudent woman. It is crucial for both partners to be loyal to each other. Fidelity is not gender-specific! Therefore, a chaste married union is a prerequisite for a loving relationship, demanded by God.

Economic Abuse

Women are economically exploited when the patriarchal society limits them to domestic and menial jobs, thus preventing self-sufficiency. Some men do not approve of their wives having jobs outside the home. Others take control of their wives' salaries, wanting them to depend entirely on them. Some cultures believe that a woman's abode is in the kitchen. This mindset has resulted in many girls not

---

[37] Bernardine Mutanu, "How Safe are your Kids from Sexual Abuse while you are Away at Work," *Daily Nation*, Nairobi October 14th, 2015, DN2 Cover Story, p. 2.

Chapter 1: The Meaning of Domestic Violence

receiving an education but instead becoming perpetual housewives. Hence, they cannot make any financial contribution to their families. President Obama declared in his speech to Kenyans on the 26th of July, 2015: "If you educate girls, they grow up to be moms. And they, because they're educated, are more likely to produce educated children."[38] He reiterated the same words in his keynote address to the African leaders at the African Union Headquarters in Addis Ababa on the 28th of July 2015:

> If you want your country to grow and succeed, you have to empower your women. The single best indicator of whether a nation will succeed is how it treats its women. When women have health care and women have education, families are stronger, communities are more prosperous, children do better in school. And when girls cannot go to school and grow up not knowing how to read or write – that denies the world future women engineers, future women doctors, future women business owners, future women presidents – that sets us all back. That's a bad tradition – not providing our girls the same education as our sons. Let Girls Learn – let girls learn so they grow up healthy and they grow up strong. And that will be good for families. And they will raise smart, healthy children, and that will be good for every one of your nations.[39]

---

[38] KTN news, Kenya.
[39] Barack Obama, "Remarks by President Obama to the People of Africa," The White House, Office of the Press Secretary, https://www.white-

Certainly, the lack of education has left some women without economic empowerment, and they lack access to their husband's financial information or bank accounts. Lack of education undermines women's potential and ability to contribute meaningfully and gainfully to society and their families. Some married women who are employed may lose their jobs when they become pregnant because their employers want them to maintain their physical appearance. Because of financial dependence and lack of support from the government, battered women continued to live in abusive relationships. Another despicable form of economic abuse is the practice of forcing a girl to marry at a tender age (as young as 10-15 years) in order for the parents to receive her bride price. On this, President Obama stated categorically that "when African girls are subjected to the mutilation of their bodies or forced into marriage at the ages of 9 or 10 or 11, that sets us back. That's not a good tradition. It needs to end."[40] Forced marriage is very archaic and should be abolished because it does not give young girls the opportunity to develop to their full potential.

It is not surprising to know that when an educated woman is economically successful, their husbands take credit for that success. Rose Uchem, a Nigerian religious sister, expresses that the patriarchal tendency has enabled men to take credit for the economic achievements of their wives and even for the bearing of children. When a woman is prosperous, people will attribute her success to the

---

house.gov/the-press-office/2015/07/28/remarks-president-obama-people-africa.

[40] Ibid.

husband with such comments: "So and so's wife achieved this," but without reference to the woman.[41] Uchem continues that this ownership trait is also expressed during traditional marriage rituals when the spokesperson of the day's events announces: "Who gives away this woman in marriage?" The intention is to call on the bride's father to formally hand over his daughter's ownership to the husband.

Apart from the marriage rituals, sometimes a woman's identity and respectability are tied to being married or not and having or not having a child. This is experienced when neighbors praise the husband: "She bore him a son." Hence, a woman does not yet "exist" until she becomes a wife or a mother of a child, and her name is replaced with "Mama Junior." An Igbo proverb illustrates explicitly the importance of a woman being married: "ugwu nwanyi bu di ya," which means that the pride of a woman is her husband. The implication of perceiving the man as the woman's pride may be problematic to an unmarried woman. Inasmuch as a woman's important status and identity reside with the husband, an unmarried woman is implicitly without honor. The intention of God at creation is for human beings to complement one another in their relationships, and not create a relationship of slavery.

Another form of economic abuse occurs when young girls are sent to hawk goods on the streets, which in turn exposes them to societal vices, such as rape and sexual assault. Often, these innocent girls do not sell only the goods they are hawking; they also sell their bodies or are drawn into such despicable acts by depraved adults. On the other hand, many young girls are forced into prostitution by their

---

[41] Uchem, 98.

parents in order to make ends meet. There are also times, especially during wars or societal conflict, when the raping of women: young and not so young, is chosen as a weapon to humiliate, degrade and demoralize the opponents. President Obama cautioned African leaders on this when he said: "Let's work together to stop sexual assault and domestic violence. Let's make clear that we will not tolerate rape as a weapon of war – it is a crime, and those who commit it must be punished. Let's lift up the next generation of women leaders who can help fight injustice, forge peace, start new businesses, create jobs, and probably hire some men. We'll all be better off when women have equal futures."[42]

Widowhood Practices and Rituals in Nigeria

The widowhood ritual is perceived as a "cleansing" phase in the life of a widow. There is the belief that the death of her dead husband contaminates a widow, and thus, her contact with other people in the community could defile them.[43] As a result of this belief, a widow is secluded from the rest of the community so that she can undergo a cleansing ritual. In many Nigerian cultures, a widow is made to shave her hair as a sign of respect for her dead husband and put on mourning clothes to appear unattractive to other men. She is forbidden to

---

[42] Obama to African Leader, August 26, 2015.
[43] Obioma and Ogbenna, 335. (This belief is somewhat abolished in many Igbo communities.)

cook. She is not allowed to eat with or care for her children.[44] These apparent isolation strategies last for two weeks or more, depending on the tradition of each community. For the community to accept that she has properly mourned the death of her husband, the widow must cry aloud at night for many weeks,[45] or sometimes cry alone in a room with the corpse. These rites affect the widow psychologically because she is treated inhumanly. However, only widows go through these rites; widowers do not. Some widows also face economic discrimination. When a man passes away, his wife automatically becomes the beneficiary of his assets. However, if a will is not written, the widow may be left without property rights or family assets. In some situations, the relatives of the deceased husband may expel the widow and withhold her late husband's assets from her. The treatment meted out to a widow is inhumane. Although Christianity is fighting to abolish this evil, educated men and women should also assist in eliminating the suffering a widow goes through at the hands of her husband's relatives.

Lady Regina Igwemezie, a Nigerian Catholic educator and headmistress, explained how cruel her widowhood experience was after the death of her husband. According to her, there were side comments and the insinuation that she was happy at the death of her husband because she did not stay at home to mourn her husband as the culture demanded. Of course, she had to arrange for the funeral ceremony of the departed husband, but the custom demanded her to

---

[44] Rosemary Edet, "Christianity and African Women's Rituals," in *The Will To Arise: Women, Tradition, and the Church in Africa*, ed. Mercy Oduyoye and Musimbi Kanyoro (Maryknoll, NY: Orbis Books, 1997), 32.
[45] Ibid.

stay indoors. She also commented on how humiliating the shaving of her hair was: "I felt very low and self-degraded, and my morale went down. I lost my confidence and could hardly even walk confidently or talk well."[46] Although women are aware that some aspects of the widowhood ritual are cruel, they are still uncomfortable to reject it, even among Christian communities. The above illustrations do not suggest that widows should not mourn the death of their husbands, but a question arises when a widower does not go through the same ritual rites.

The abuse experienced by many women in various parts of Africa indicates one thing: women are still perceived and treated as second-class citizens.

Effects of Abuse on Children

It goes without saying that when the goats are eating grass, the kids are looking at their mouths. Children are very vulnerable and innocent. They perceive their parents as the perfect examples to emulate. When a child watches his or her father abuse and physically assault the mother, that child may be inclined to practice the same behavior in the future, especially when said child does not go through a counseling process. This hostile behavior, apparently, will turn into bullying, antagonistic, brutal, destructive, and vicious lifestyle, especially when that child is not counseled. It is on record that

---

[46] Regina Igwemezie, "Widowhood: A Harrowing Experience," Unpublished Monograph (ISBN: 978-2643-96-13 Anambra, Nigeria: 2005), 17, 23.

children who are raised in an abusive environment and who are abused sexually end up becoming more violent, fearful, and mistrustful.

The story of Alice told above is a good example to illustrate this traumatic experience. Alice is ten years old this year, and the trauma of the experience of rape continues to haunt her even after many counseling sessions. The *Daily Nations* reported that Alice cannot walk to school alone and she cannot go anywhere unaccompanied. When she sees a man approaching, she will run and hide. She also gets frightened when she approaches the place where she was defiled and cannot pass by the place unaccompanied. She screams at night because of nightmares of the experience.[47] What a tragic and heartbreaking way to live!

Children who experience abuse are also prone to anger, to show aggressive behavior in schools, religious communities, and at home, and to have thoughts about suicide.[48] Surprisingly, some parents condemn their children for becoming aggressive when these children are only living out what they learned from them.

In her work *Psychological Counselling for Africa*, Elizabeth Okpalaenwe, a Catholic religious Sister and Psychologist, narrated a story of how Tita, who had watched her father abuse her mother, became very violent and a sadist. She takes delight in bullying her younger ones, and eating their food, and none of them could complain to their mother because they fear being tortured or tormented by her afterward. Tita abandoned school and went to be trained as a

---

[47] Mutanu, Daily Nation, DN2, P. 2.
[48] Ose, 5.

policewoman. At the training camp, they found her to be too brutal. As luck would have it, the night Tita planned to kill her mother, she was awake, and her mother confessed her true love for her: "My daughter, I care about you. I truly love you." This brought transformation and reconciliation as Tita confessed: "No one has ever shown me love since I was born. You and my dad detested and fought with each other all the time. All we learned from him was violence, sad mood, and hatred."[49] Tita's healing started when mother and daughter told their stories to each other of how everything started. Tita began to accept her mother's love and was transformed.

Another interesting story was told of a frail old man who went to live with his son, daughter-in-law, and four-year-old grandson. The old man's hands trembled, his eyesight was blurred, and his step faltered. The family ate together at the table. But the elderly grandfather's shaky hands and failing sight made eating difficult. Peas rolled off his spoon onto the floor. When he grasped the glass filled with milk, it spilled on the tablecloth. The son and daughter-in-law became irritated with the mess. "We must do something about father," said the son. "I've had enough of his spilled milk, noisy eating, and food on the floor," the wife responded.

So, the husband and wife set a small table at the corner. There, Grandfather ate alone while the rest of the family enjoyed dinner. Since Grandfather had broken a dish or two, his food was served in a wooden bowl. When the family glanced in Grandfather's direction,

---

[49] Elizabeth N. Okpalaenwe, *Psychological Counselling for Africa: Handbook on Psychotherapy and Cultural Counselling in African Contexts* (Nigeria, Onitsha: Laurans Prints, 2014), 94-95.

sometimes he had tears in his eyes as he sat alone. Still, the only words the couple had for him were sharp admonitions when he dropped a fork or spilled food.

Their four-year-old child watched it all in silence. One evening before supper, the father noticed his son playing with wood scraps on the floor. He asked the child sweetly, "What are you making?" Just as sweetly, the boy responded: "Oh, I am making a little bowl for you and Mum to eat your food from when I grow up." The child smiled and went back to work. His words struck the parents speechless.

Then tears started to stream down their cheeks. Though no word was spoken, both knew what had to be done. That evening, the husband took Grandfather's hand and gently led him back to the family table. For the remainder of his days, he ate every meal with the family. After that, neither husband nor wife seemed to care any longer when a fork was dropped, milk spilled, or the tablecloth soiled.[50]

These stories illustrate how the violent behavior of parents or their values can shape and affect the value of an innocent child. Children are always curious and remarkably perceptive; their eyes, ears, and minds actively absorb and process the information they receive. When they see their parents providing a happy home, they will exhibit this attitude all their lives. That is why a child's development can be positively or negatively affected depending on the environment that nurtures the child. Both nature and nurture play an important role in a child's development. A Developmental Psychologist and Psychoanalyst, Erik Erikson's psychosocial stages of human

---

[50] Ranjan De Silva, *A Better Way to Sell: Mastery of Sales Through Mastery of Self* (India: Dorling Kindersley Ltd, 2009), 13 &14.

development[51] bring to light that the experiences of consistent affection and love from parents help a child to develop trust in his parents and the world. However, a child who witnesses or experiences violence, rejection, sexual abuse, and a hostile environment lives in fear, insecurity, anxiety, and guilt and finds it hard to trust.

Therefore, if the challenges of this trauma are not resolved through counseling, the child may end up lacking self-confidence, being very aggressive, feeling insecure, and having a pessimistic outlook on life and the world. Imagine a tree seedling without sunlight, sufficient watering, and nourishing manure to nurture and support its growth into a healthy tree. It will be adversely affected, and the tree will not grow properly. Likewise, children need to be nurtured with love and support from their parents for proper development, rather than with hatred, abuse, and violence.

Catalyst of Domestic Violence

The abuse that some women face is often rooted in the misconception of the patriarchal system, leading to women being falsely regarded as the property of men.[52] Some women suffer oppression and subordination as men exert influence over them. Women are to be seen and not to be heard, and their main function is to procreate children, preferably male children. The patriarchal authority naturally and socially empowers the man to admonish, reprimand, and

---

[51] Barbara Engler, *Personality Theories*, 9th Ed. (Belmont, CA: Cengage Learning Publishers, 2013), 140.

[52] Obioma and Ogbenna, 330.

punish anyone in his family who resists his attempt to control and protect. As the man owns and rules over his family, the mother nurtures the children. When he has a tough day at work or outside the home, he comes home and asserts his authority over his wife and children. Sometimes, this cycle of violence sets off a series of events within the family: the husband may hit his wife, who is unable to retaliate, so she ends up hitting the children. The older, stronger children might then resort to hitting their younger siblings.

Des-Obi Obioma and Boniface Ogbenna (Nigerian Catholic Priests) present many examples where women are relegated to a lower position in society: a woman sits on the left-hand side of the man in order to wait appropriately on the man, and in return, the man shields and protects her from attack. The marriage rituals may also suggest one fact: a man is considered the head of the family, while a woman is seen as subordinate and unequal in dignity. This belief is symbolized by the woman's kneeling before the man and presenting him with wine, a ritual that is meant to solemnize the union. And finally, after the wedding, the woman changes her name to the man's name.[53]

These cultural practices are not inherently bad, but they may encourage a sense of superiority and ownership over women in men. Apparently, some married men will overlook the positive aspects of a patriarchal structure, exercise dominating power over their spouses, and set boundaries and rules for the women to obey just for the thrill of it. Such an attitude or approach in marriage does not sow

---

[53] Obioma and Ogbenna. 331. See also D. A. Lane, "Christian Feminism," *The Furrow* 36, no. 11 (1985): 664.

harmony, and no sane woman opts for such a life of misery in the name of marital commitment.

The superior attitude of men starts with the preference of a child's sex in the family to the way children are socialized. When a boy in a family receives an abundance of love and is treated as special, he develops a positive self-image, a strong sense of security, and self-assurance. The girl, however, who was raised to be a homemaker and treated differently from her brother, may end up feeling insecure, weak, and fearful. Children must receive equal love and support from their parents to develop good self-esteem and confidence.

In most African countries, a male child is more appreciated than a female one. In some Igbo cultures, a male child is a sign of posterity for the community. Thus, at the birth of a male child, both men and women rejoice with joy, singing "Onye ji egbe bia ngaa," which means he who has a gun, let him come.[54] Gun, in this case, represents power, autonomy, and manliness. On the other hand, when a female child is born, the women only rejoice with a song: "Onye ji ego bia ngaa," which means he who has wealth, let him come. The typical expectation among Igbo parents is to receive a bride price for their daughters from their prospective sons-in-law. This implies that female children are seen only as a form of wealth by their parents and are, therefore, considered second-class citizens. Nevertheless, this culture is evolving and changing in some Igbo societies as some women are more involved in caregiving for their parents in their old age than men.

---

[54] Nwachukwu-Udaku, 115.

In some Kenyan cultures, boys are traditionally taught that they are superior to girls during socialization/initiation ceremonies. As a result, they often treat their sisters as subordinates, even if the sister is older. This is experienced immediately after the circumcision ceremony when the newly circumcised young men acquire a new status in society and live in a separate house. In most families, young boys are allowed to air their views on family matters, while women and girls are expected to be in the kitchen. Nonetheless, this idea is changing in some educated families, and girls are given equal opportunities.

Additionally, young men are socialized to repress their feelings and taught by their fathers or uncles that "real men do not cry like women and children." The patriarchal culture inculcates in them aggressive behavior as well as exercises dominant power in family life and decision-making. This superior attitude of young men promotes social inequality between males and females in society. Most young men project this autocratic power when there is a misunderstanding between two male friends, especially when derogatory words are used. One is likely to hear this phrase: "Do not talk to me like that; I am not a woman."[55]

Furthermore, most parents persistently keep a closer watch over their adolescent girls while allowing young boys to come and go at will due to the perception of girls as more fragile than their male counterparts. Sometimes, only boys are sent to school while girls remain at home to learn housekeeping skills, preparing them for motherhood. Consequently, the lack of education for some girls leads to

---

[55] Uchem, 83.

economic dependence on their future husbands. Clarke explains that "women are taught by their parents and society that their worth is based on their physical beauty and appeal to men rather than their creative responses to life situations. Hence, the girls learn to be more passive than boys."[56]

With this kind of orientation, many young men become very authoritarian in their leadership style and in their behavior within the family unit, while women are more empathetic, compassionate, kind-hearted, and passive. As a result of patriarchal socialization, some men regard their wives not as equal partners in their marital life but rather as unequal spouses to be controlled and marginalized.

This dysfunctional practice embedded in the patriarchal system is changing in this digital era when educated women in high positions are competing and challenging men in different fields and professions. Okpalaenwe captured this point well when she explains that, "Men have failed to realize that their strength lies mainly in physical prowess, but when there is something that requires determination to succeed, women hardly give up the challenge."[57] She explained further how Mercy was ridiculed because she wanted to study medicine. It was unheard of for women to study medicine; their profession was nursing for caregiving purposes. But through determination and hard work, Mercy excelled, and her dream came true.

Additionally, poverty, illiteracy, and unemployment can lead to an escalation of domestic violence. Poverty is a state of living in

---

[56] Clarke, 39.
[57] Okpalaenwe, 66.

destitution, penury, and want. It is a situation where one lacks basic needs due to insufficient resources. Illiteracy is a state of not knowing how to read and write, i.e., lack of education, while unemployment is a state where a jobless but eligible person remains unhired. These three conditions can intersect because illiteracy can lead to unemployment, which in turn can lead to poverty. This does not mean that an uneducated person cannot work hard to escape from poverty or that domestic violence occurs mostly among the poor. No, domestic violence cuts across classes and cultures. Poverty is not always the cause of abuse. For example, some wealthy men abuse their partners, while some poor couples live happily together. In fact, the person inflicting harm makes a conscious choice to do so.

The point I am trying to make is that these three conditions can create opportunities for hostile and aggressive behavior in the family. For instance, when a man loses his job or his business collapses, he becomes antagonistic and sees himself as a failure. A hungry man, they say, is an angry man. When there is no food on the table, he can become frustrated and aggressive. When a woman, because of illiteracy, does not know her rights, she cannot fight for her right to human dignity, and thus, she remains in an abusive relationship. During his address to a Colloquium that was held in Rome on the theme "The Complementarity of Man and Woman in Marriage," Pope Francis agreed that poverty could lead to a crisis in the family. He commented: "In our day, marriage and the family are in crisis. We now live in a culture of the temporary, in which more and more people are simply giving up on marriage as a public commitment.... Evidence is mounting that the decline of the marriage culture is associated with increased poverty and a host of other social ills, disproportionately affecting women, children, and the elderly. It is always they who suffer the most in this crisis."[58]

In my ministry with the victims of abuse, I noticed that the majority of them were poor. Unfortunately, they remained in abusive relationships for long because they could not get good jobs. Those who were educated among them had quit their jobs and were under financial stress. However, they received help when they could say "NO" to their helpless situation and ran to the shelter for support. Sometimes, the lack of material comfort can lead destitute individuals, particularly vulnerable girls and women, to use what they have to obtain what they need. It also pushes women who are economically handicapped to seek ways to sustain themselves and their children, especially when the man of the house cares less about his family. It can also result in human trafficking and sexual exploitation of vulnerable girls. Sometimes, sexual abuse takes place in extreme poverty situations when a girl is used as a means to an end.

Okpalaenwe captures this well when she explains how girls take to the streets at night to fend for their families, who are living from hand to mouth. She tells the story of how a girl whose parents were dead and her uncle used her as a sex object took to the street to cater for the well-being of her grandmother and herself. The abused girl explained: "At least men give you 10 or 20 bucks if you meet a generous guy after they are done with you. Many of them are very violent. They talk to you disrespectfully and sometimes refuse to pay the

---

[58] Pope Francis, "Marriage and the Family are in Crisis," Vatican Radio, en.radiovaticana.va/news/2014/11/17/pope_francis_marriage_and_the_family_are_in_crisis/1111371.

agreed amount once the work is completed." When asked whether the grandmother is aware that she goes out at night for prostitution; she responded: "Yes, that is the only way she can eat, and my child, too."[59] This despicable, ugly, and unfortunate situation is the fate of many women. There are many decent women who are forced into the sex business because of poverty and economic hardship.

All these conditions and more could pave the way for the abuse of women to remain unabated. However, it is time for women to arise and say: "Enough is enough!" The will to arise among women is in line with the story that I read from Wisdom 101. One day all the employees reached the office and saw a big piece of advice written on the door. "Yesterday, the person who has been sabotaging the success of so many in this company passed away. You are invited to join the funeral." In the beginning, they were sad about the death of one of their colleagues, but after a while, they became curious to know who compromised their growth. Everyone thought: "Well, at least the one who stopped my progress died!" One by one, the thrilled and excited employees got closer to the coffin, and when they looked inside, they were speechless. They stood shocked in silence as if someone had touched the deepest part of their soul. There was a mirror inside the coffin, and everyone who looked inside could see him/herself. A sign beside the mirror read: "There is only one person capable of setting limits to your growth... It is you."[60]

The strength and determination to overcome the feeling of helplessness associated with domestic violence partly stems from the

---

[59] Okpalaenwe, 99-102.
[60] Gupte, 28.

victims' awareness and willingness to surpass their limiting beliefs. It is essential for them to realize that they are responsible for their lives and to take control of them.

This chapter has presented the meaning of domestic abuse, the different kinds of abuse that women encounter, the experiences of violence among some African women, the effects of violence on children, and the catalyst for violent behavior and abuse. Certainly, discarding a tradition that does not promote equal interpersonal relationships in families will allow for the authentic life that Christ promised, "I came so that they might have life and have it more abundantly" (John 10:10). Some cultural practices are not life-giving, e.g., female genital mutilation, forced widow inheritance, child marriage, preventing girls from going to school and forcing them into marriage. In light of this, could creating a forum for teens and young adults in a Christian setting where sexual issues are discussed reduce the immoral behavior that is plaguing the world? We understand that suggesting that a woman's primary place is in the kitchen is a sensitive issue. Therefore, could sharing household chores reduce power struggles between spouses? After all, marriage is a vocation of mutual love, support, maturity, and maintaining a harmonious relationship.

It is not enough to uncover the problem; there's also a need for a solution. The woman who suffers abuse needs care that can bring healing and reconciliation to her humanity and her dignity. Her suffering is made possible by the injustice in the world, and this injustice is to be challenged and confronted since they feel helpless sometimes. Jeffery Means, a pastor, believes that the victims of abuse feel powerless and hopeless in their situation. For them, nothing can be done unless God intervenes and provides a solution, and since God does not intervene, they conclude that God does not care. Means concludes that this suffering is open to human intervention to stop and prevent it.[61] The victims of abuse need to regain their distorted dignity. Many documents of the Church uphold the dignity of women and condemn the exploitation of women. It is to these documents to which this work will now turn.

---

[61] Jeffrey Means, *Trauma and Evil: Healing the Wounded Soul* (Minneapolis, MN: Augsburg Fortress, 2000), 27.

Chapter 2

The Church's Teaching on the Dignity of Women

> A gracious woman gets honor....
> but a cruel man hurts himself.
>
> - Proverb 11:16-17

Within the Church, many official documents uphold the dignity of women, but scarcely do the documents treat the problem of domestic violence. Marie Giblin confesses that the Church is relatively silent in its official teachings on domestic violence, and sometimes, its statements treat violence against women as a problem of secular society.[1] This is evidenced when, in 2009, the South African Bishops Conference highlighted that substance abuse has an enormous impact on domestic violence and suggested that the police should be trained in the handling of domestic violence cases. They stressed that the police should also maintain a register that would reflect reported incidences of violence.[2] These suggestions are certainly helpful. Nevertheless, the Church could also play a pastoral and active role in combating this evil. Pope Francis, on the 7th of February 2015,

---

[1] Marie Giblin, "Catholic Church Teaching and Domestic Violence," Listening: *Journal of Religion and Culture*, no. 34 (Jan 1999): 10.

[2] Lois Law, "Implementation of the Domestic Violence Act 116 of 1998," South African Catholic Bishop's Conference Parliamentary Liaison Office, October 16, 2009, http://d2zmx6m-lqh7g3a.doudfront.net/cdn/farfuture/mtime:1259069738/files/docs/091028sacbc_0.pdf.

condemned domestic violence against women and female genital mutilation and called them degradation that had to be combated because they reduced women to mere objects.³ Jeffery Means also noticed that the prayerful support of the Church is felt enormously when Christians are suffering because of death, sickness, natural disaster, etc., but the same response is not experienced for someone who is suffering at the hands of human-induced trauma such as violence.⁴ The Church needs to create more avenues for the awareness of this evil and how it is eating deep into the fabric of family life.

Some documents of the Church, e.g., *Gaudium et spes* (Pastoral Constitution on the Church in the Modern World, 1965), discuss the problems of the marital union as polygamy, divorce, selfishness, hedonism, unlawful contraceptive practices, and population expansion with no mention of domestic violence (no. 47). However, some documents of the Church support the dignity of women. The document of John Paul II, *Familiaris consortio* (On the Family, 1981), talks about the dignity of women and how they have become objects of trade (no. 24). He writes: "Unfortunately the Christian message about the dignity of women is contradicted by that persistent mentality which considers the human being not as a person but as a thing, as an object of trade, at the service of selfish interest and mere

---

[3] Pope Francis, "Pope Condemns Female Mutilation, Domestic Violence Against Women," *The Nation*, February 8th, 2015.

[4] Jeffery Means, *Trauma and Evil: Healing the Wounded Soul* (Minneapolis, MN: Augsburg Fortress, 2000), 28.

pleasure: the first victims of this mentality are women."⁵ In African society, such transactions could be the bride price ritual.

In many African societies, a marital union is not recognized as legal until the bride's price is paid. When a woman leaves her husband to another man, her dowry is completely refunded by the second man to the former husband. If the bride price is not refunded, any child the second man begets with the woman belongs to the first husband.⁶ Thus, the payment of the bride price by a man makes a woman legally married to him. Bride price is culturally accepted, and it is valuable to the extent that it shows the commitment of the bridegroom. However, this culture is questionable when it becomes a means to purchase and acquire a marriageable bride. The sociologists Oyediran and Isiugo-Abanihe explain that "upon marriage, a woman surrenders to her husband the exclusive sexual rights and obedience." These two professors believe that this exclusive right gives a man the liberty to violate and batter his wife if he feels that she has not adequately fulfilled her obligation.⁷ Dowry payment is a symbol of commitment to the union, not a tool to control a woman's sexual life.

---

⁵ John Paul II, *Familiaris consortio*, Libreria Editrice Vaticana, December 15, 1981, http://www.vatican.va/holy_father/john_paul_ii/apost_exhortations/documents/hf_jp-ii_exh_19811122_familiaris-consortio_en.html, no. 24.

⁶ Edmund Ilogu, *Christianity and Ibo Culture* (Leiden, Netherland: E.J. Brill, 1974), 28-29.

⁷ Kolawole Oyediran and Uche Isiugo-Abanihe, "Perceptions of Nigerian Women on Domestic Violence: Evidence from 2003 Nigeria Demographic and Health Survey," *African Journal of Reproductive Health* 9, no. 2 (August 2005): 39.

Sexual union is the giving of the entire person – body and spirit – to each other and accepting the same from each other. Unfortunately, coercive sexual activity dominates many marriages rather than sexual activity and companionship that promote mutual submission and self-giving love by spouses.[8] Submission can be tolerated when it is mutual and when St. Paul's letter to the Ephesians is correctly interpreted: "Be subject to one another out of reverence for Christ" (Eph 5:21). St. John Paul II calls this submission, "Bi-subjectivity." In his *Theology of the Body*, John Paul II explains that bi-subjectivity is at the basis of one single body of the married couple who are called to love each other just as Christ loves his Body, the Church.[9] Husbands and wives are meant to love each other equally and be submissive to one another. They are of one body, of equal nature, apart from the obvious biological differences, and they share the same nature created in God's image. Thus, mutual respect and dignity are the keys to healthy interpersonal relationships devoid of crises and abuse.

Another document of the Church that promotes the dignity of women is the *Letter to Women* by John Paul II. He writes:

> Women's dignity has often been unacknowledged, and their prerogatives misrepresented; they have often been relegated

---

[8] Austin Flannery, ed. *Gaudium et spes*, Vatican Council II, The Conciliar and Post Conciliar Documents (Boston, MA: St. Paul Books and Media, 1992), no. 49.

[9] John Paul II, "*Theology of the Body*," August 25, 1982, Eternal Word Television Network, www.ewtn.com/library/papaldoc/jp2tbind.htm, no. 91.

to the margins of society and even reduced to servitude. This has prevented women from truly being themselves, and it has resulted in spiritual impoverishment of humanity. Certainly, it is no easy task to assign the blame for this, considering the many kinds of cultural conditioning that have shaped ways of thinking and acting over the centuries. And if objective blame, especially in particular historical contexts, has belonged to not just a few members of the Church, for this I am truly sorry.[10]

This letter is a right step towards a right direction, although it is silent on the issues about domestic abuse. However, it supports the dignity of women and expresses remorse on what women have faced in the history of the Church and the world. It acknowledges the fact that women have been subjected to all kinds of hardship in history, which is against the divine will of God, who created a man and a woman as equal beings. For instance, St. Augustine of Hippo declares that "a woman apart from a man is not made in the image of God, whereas a man apart from a woman is."[11] Both males and females are created in God's image; thus, spouses are equal partners in the marital union since their union reflects God's love and is a sign of the union between Christ and the Church. St. John Paul II clarifies that authentic marital love requires a man to have a profound respect for

---

[10] John Paul II, "*Letter of John Paul II to Women*," Libreria Editrice Vaticana, June 29, 1995, http://www.vatican.va/holy_father/john_paul_ii/letters/documents/hf_jp-ii_let_29061995_women_en.html, no. 3.

[11] Mercy Oduyoye, *Daughters of Anowa: African Women and Patriarchy* (Maryknoll, NY: Orbis Books, 1999), 5.

the equal dignity of his wife. Quoting St. Ambrose, John Paul II admonishes the men: "You are not her master, but her husband. She was not given to you to be your slave, but your wife."[12] This statement is so powerful and needs to be heard by all African men and women so that women will be treated with dignity and respect.

Furthermore, the Catholic Bishops Conference of Nigeria on February 20, 2002, also issued a pastoral letter entitled "Restoring the Dignity of the Nigerian Woman," where they condemned the abuse women face through the trafficking of Nigerian women to the Western world for prostitution.[13] The letter explains that over 15,000 Nigerian women engage in prostitution in Italy alone. It blamed the problem of prostitution on poverty, illiteracy, unemployment, criminal networks, greed, abdication of parental responsibility, and moral degeneracy. Probably, some Nigerian girls, who are victims of human trafficking, could have been saved if this letter had been judiciously preached about in their local churches. Unfortunately, pastoral letters are sometimes only for clerics, religious, and a few learned lay faithful.

Saint Pope John Paul II's excellent addresses on what he called the "Theology of the Body"[14] are worth reflecting upon.

---

[12] John Paul II, *Familiaris consortio*, no. 25.

[13] Catholic Bishops Conference of Nigeria, *Restoring the Dignity of the Nigerian Woman* (Lagos, Nigeria: Sovereign Ventures, 2002), 2

[14] John Paul II. "Theology of the Body," Eternal Word Television Network, August 25, 1982, www.ewtn.com/library/papaldoc/jp2tbind.htm

Chapter 2: The Church's Teaching on the Dignity of Women

The Theology of the Body (TOB)

In his one hundred and twenty-nine Wednesday audiences, Pope St. John Paul II addressed the purpose of our existence, the dignity of the human person, the importance of our sexuality, as well as the need to uphold and affirm the other person so that the other will not be a means to an end but rather an equal creature of God. Both a man and woman are equal, created in God's image. Ultimately, male and female God created them (Genesis. 1:27), for God's self and for each other. They share a common humanity despite their biological differences. These differences form the foundation of their covenantal union – the mutual freedom and love in procreation and raising of children. In exploring this image of God, Pope explains: "Man became the 'image and likeness' of God not only through his own humanity, but also through the communion of persons which man and woman form right from the beginning" (TOB, Nov 14, 1979, no. 3). Certainly, the communion of persons takes place when the husband and wife give themselves to each other in mutual self-giving love. In other words, each gives out the entire person – body and spirit – to another and accepts the same from another. This union reflects God's love, and it is a sign of union between Christ and the Church, who lays down his life for his friends (John 15:13).

The Theology of the Body presents the importance of the physical body. In explaining this Biblical phrase, "the man and his wife were both naked, yet they felt no shame" (Genesis 2:25); the Pope emphasizes that this innocence is the mutual experience of welcoming and accepting the other as a gift. However, shame only entered when the other was treated as "an object for myself or an object of lust and misappropriation" (TOB, Feb 6, 1980, nos. 2-3). If the physical body bears the image of God, why is it treated sometimes as an object of ridicule and a thing to be used or abused? Many times, the abusers blame Satan/sin when they treat their wives as objects to be used rather than persons to love and respect. Rather than blaming sin, the abuser should be responsible for his violent actions since he has the freedom to choose not to abuse others. The physical body is to be treated as a sign of the image of God since as embodied souls we live our humanity through our bodies. We express our love for God, self, and others through our bodies, and it is in our bodies that we are connected with the Incarnate Word. It was St. Athanasius of Alexandria who puts it well that the Word was made flesh, so that we might be made gods. In other words, the Divine became human and we were deified through his human nature, and so we become divines. For the fact that the Incarnate Word became like us, our physical body is no longer a thing to be seen as evil or unimportant. Gone are the days when a woman's body was seen as evil, a disease that requires a cure, and a serious obstacle to the path of salvation for men.[15] Both a man and a woman bear the image of God in their humanity and also in their communitarian relationship. St. John Paul II writes: "The human body bore in itself, in the mystery of creation, an unquestionable sign of the image of God" (TOB, May 14, 1980, no. 3).

---

[15] Barbara H. Andolsen, "Whose Sexuality? Whose Tradition? Women, Experience and Roman Catholic Sexual Ethics," in Readings in Moral Theology, No. 9: Feminist Ethics and the Catholic Moral Tradition, ed. Charles Curran, Margaret Farley, and Richard McCormick (New York, NY: Paulist Press, 1996), 211.

The gospel message of love that St. John Paul II preached in the *Theology of the Body* is very radical and important to every family. It portrays the equality of all human beings, whom God created male and female. It is unfortunate that sometimes the headship of a man in the family (Ephesians 5:21) is misinterpreted: "Be subordinate to one another out of reverence for Christ." The husband is to be the chief servant like Christ, and the wife will respond with loving submission as the Church does to Christ. It is difficult for this interpersonal relationship to exist in the midst of violence. The questions that arise are: How may the Church minister to people who dominate in relationships and also those who suffer the effects of this oppression? Since human beings cannot live without love, how will women become more fulfilled and regarded as equal partners in loving marital relationships?

The inequality between partners is fearfully and silently expressed when some women are reluctant to vote for another woman in the political arena, when some women lack the courage to express their views on issues that concern them in society, when most women fear facing problems regarding landed property; when they are afraid to talk about the denial of the right to inherit their father's land or manage their late husband's estate/business. These fears are genuine since the process of socialization promotes an unequal spirit and attitude, as expressed above. The question this fear evokes is: What can each family and community do to transform the method of socialization in our society so that young girls can find their rightful places in society among the opposite sex? How may the Church help in the crises facing many families today? The Catholic Bishops gathered for the three-week synod on the family at St. Peter's Basilica in the Vatican, which was opened with a Mass on Sunday, the 4th of October 2015, by Pope Francis. I hoped this synod would deal effectively with the problems of family life, especially domestic violence.

This chapter explains and clarifies that some Church documents promote women's dignity. However, the Church can pastorally help women regain their rights and be respected in their families and in society. On another note, the Church can aid abused women who are wounded to regain their dignity. When there is a problem in the family, it ultimately affects the whole Church since the family is the domestic church. Of course, some Church documents observed that families face enormous crises. St. John Paul II in *Gratissimam sane* (Letter to Families, 1994) stated that profound crises threaten family life, and he advised that "help can be sought at marriage and family counseling centers, where it is possible, among other things, to obtain the assistance of specifically trained psychologists and psychotherapists" (no. 7). The Nigerian Bishops also noted that "families today face the multiple crises of violence and crime, which include child abuse, prostitution, and women trafficking due to erosion of family values and the sacredness of life."[16] If the domestic church is facing profound crises, what strategy can be used to combat the problem? The woman who suffers abuse needs pastoral care that can bring healing and reconciliation to her humanity since her dignity is distorted by the abuse and domination she receives at home. It is on this reconciliation that this work will focus in the next chapter.

---

[16] Catholic Bishops Conference of Nigeria, "Towards Sustaining our Democracy," *Catholic Online*, September 25, 2006, http://cathoilc.org/national/national_story.php?id=21375.

Chapter 3

Toward a Genuine Reconciliation Process

"The Lord's servant must not be quarrelsome but kind to everyone and correcting his opponents with gentleness."

- 2 Timothy 2:24-25

The word reconciliation is often used in our society – in the political, social, spiritual, cultural, and business worlds. Reconciliation is sought after when people in a community or family are not getting along well, when the pain of war and its aftermath is staring us in the face, and we are seeking peace. It is also sought after when spouses are in a strained relationship, when friends lose connection, when the relationship with God is broken, etc. We live in a broken society. When one reads the newspaper, listens to the television or radio, or searches the social network, one will likely discover ample news of broken relationships and how to restore them. Because of our experiences of brokenness, we all need reconciliation.

My interest in an authentic reconciliation process among victims of violence started in 2010 during my ministerial experience in the US, at a transitional safe home for abused women and their children. These women desire reconciliation with their partners, but the process is rushed and elusive. Generally, human beings have the tendency and desire to fix material things. Consequently, conflict can also be fixed just as a broken car is fixed in the garage (or by an auto mechanic). To fix the conflict, the reconcilers sometimes use the wrong approach, wrong timing, and wrong people. The reconcilers are quick to persuade the victims and the perpetrators of violence to accept that violence is evil and to end the conflict; however, they are impatient to gradually open the wounds of the past hurt that could impede the reconciliation process. The reconcilers may not be properly trained in handling cases of abuse or even the reconciliation process. The victims may end up becoming more hurt, unruly, headstrong, and recalcitrant rather than allowing healing and forgiveness to take place.

In light of the different ways through which women are abused in our African culture, the question remains: How may the Church confront this form of violence and the suffering it causes through a genuine reconciliation process? Can reconciliation end violence since some people, after exchanging hugs, still go back to violent tendencies? What religious, social-cultural, or political structures can be put in place to sustain the process of reconciliation? Certainly, when the proper way of reconciling people is followed, those needing it will experience healing and forgiveness and may not go back to their violent way of life.

This chapter proposes that the reconciliation models of Robert Schreiter can develop in the Church and African society a sense of justice toward women who experience abuse. The chapter will also clarify what reconciliation is, the ineffective methods of the reconciliation process, the relationship between violence and reconciliation, and how violent behavior distorts the victims of abuse's true story, as well as the true reconciliation process. By illuminating what reconciliation is not, the Church leaders, pastoral workers, and those seeking an authentic reconciliation journey will discover how to provide one effectively and how to respond to domestic abuse cases.

Robert Schreiter is a Catholic priest of the Missionaries of the Precious Blood and a professor of Historical and Doctrinal Studies at Catholic Theological Union Chicago. He is an internationally recognized expert in the theology of reconciliation and has published many books and articles on the spirituality of reconciliation and peacebuilding.[1] This work will use his many theories and writings, especially *Reconciliation: Mission and Ministry in a Changing Social Order*, to explain the dynamics of reconciliation from a Christian perspective.

Meaning of Genuine Reconciliation

According to the online dictionary, reconciliation is the restoration of friendly relations. The etymology of the word is from the old French word *reconcilier*, which is directly from the Latin word *reconcilare*, meaning: "to bring together, regain, win over again, concili-

---

[1] Some of his works include: *The Ministry of Reconciliation: Spirituality and Strategies* published by Orbis Books in 1998; "The Ministry of Forgiveness in a Praxis of Reconciliation," An international seminar on reconciliation given at Lima in 2006; "Reconciliation and Healing as a Paradigm for Mission," *International Review of Mission* 94, (Jan 2005): 74-83; In *Water and In Blood: A Spirituality of Solidarity and Hope*, NY: Crossroad, 1988, "Liturgy

"As Reconciling," *Liturgical Ministry* 17, no. 3 (Sum 2008): 139-145; "Reconciliation as a Missionary Task," *Missiology* 20, no. 1 (Jan 1992): 3-10.

ate."² Reconciliation is the process of restoring a broken relationship to establish peace and unity. It is an act that brings two or more former adversaries or rivalries together into relationships. For Schreiter, true reconciliation brings healing, frees the victim and the abuser, and involves the restoration of the dignity and respect of the victim. According to June Hunt, reconciliation is the act of restoring or harmonizing differences between one another.³

Reconciliation is not only about addressing the injustice in the community, trying to extinguish the flames of disagreement, conflict mediation or resolution, or advocating for peace among conflicting interests; it is what God does. Therefore, it is a gift from God, although human beings must desire to reconcile. A good example of the reconciliation process in the Scripture is the reconciliation process between Joseph and his brothers in Genesis 37:2-45:15. Joseph, having been sold by his brothers, was elevated by God. Thinking that Joseph had died, these brothers did not recognize him when they came to Egypt in search of food. When the process of reconciliation started, Joseph forgave and reconciled with his brothers.

Certainly, it is crucial for the victim of abuse to go through the process of reconciliation in order to begin the process of healing and letting go of the traumatic experiences and not necessarily to restore the broken relationship. The reason is that the abuser might refuse to admit, minimize, or deny the sin he has committed; nevertheless, the abused has to seek healing and reconciliation with herself and with

---

[2] Online Etymology Dictionary, www.etymonline.com/index.php?term=reconcile.

[3] June Hunt, *Reconciliation: Restoring Broken Relationships* (Torrance, CA: Rose Publication, 2014), 3.

Chapter 3: Toward a Genuine Reconciliation Process

God. Sometimes, broken relationships are never restored even after forgiveness and healing have taken place because of the betrayed trust, while some relationships are never the same again, even after going through the process of reconciliation.

Schreiter believes that reconciliation is not repentance. While repentance means confronting the wrong done, confessing it as sin, and taking appropriate steps necessary for change, reconciliation begins with the healing of the victim through God's grace. Furthermore, repentance originates from the perpetrators of violence; reconciliation and forgiveness come from the victim of violence[4] who needs to break the chains of betrayal and the trauma of abuse in order to be healed, especially when the abuser does not acknowledge the violence as sin. Reconciliation is not only about healing the wounds of the victim and the forgiveness of the perpetrators of evil; it is also about transforming the social structures that have promoted and sustained violence.

Reconciliation may not take place without the victim and the abuser coming to the awareness that violence is a sin and that violence has brutal consequences for the abused. No one can actually seek reconciliation when both the abused and the abuser think that no wrong has been done. Of course, some African men do not see domestic violence as a sin. Some think that violent behavior toward their wives is their right since women are their property. Others perceive violence as an acceptable way to live a married life and to exercise control as the head of the family. This telling comment was made

---

[4] Robert Schreiter, *Reconciliation: Mission and Ministry in a Changing Social Order* (Maryknoll, NY: Orbis Books, 1992), 21

by a man in my community in Abia State of Nigeria when asked why he physically abused his wife: "Anam ahazi ego m;" which means, "I am shaping and organizing my finances." Similarly, some African women seemingly approve of wife-battering, as explained in the first chapter, as a sign of love since a man cannot guard his wife jealously unless he loves her. Reconciliation asks these questions: How do we confront violence? How do we come to terms with the suffering that violence causes and liberate the victim through a genuine reconciliation process? When domestic violence or wife battering is accepted in a society, how may reconciliation take place? Reconciliation certainly is meaningless when violence is condoned. However, when violence against women is perceived as a sin, then there can be a movement toward a reconciliation process, but, first, we have to understand the relationship between reconciliation and violence.

Relationship between Reconciliation and Violence

Humans are fragile beings who live in an unstable culture and society. Sometimes, we feel uncertain and insecure. To avoid perishing in fear, we need to discover who we are to experience a sense of safety and selfhood.[5] Schreiter suggests that we discover our identity through rituals; that is, we assign meanings to events and physical features in our lives through stories. It is from the stories of our parents that we learned where we were born: the time, season, date, month, and year, the circumstances surrounding our birth, and the

---

[5] Schreiter, 1992, 31.

names we were given. From them, we also become aware of our siblings, extended relatives, our village, tribe, nationality, etc.

These stories help us to understand that we are humans who are wonderfully made, that we are created equal and unique in God's image, that the universe is interconnected and interdependent, and that our stories are part of the universal story. The story of our uniqueness and history explains the true story of each human person. It makes us human and gives us a sense of security and selfhood. In sharing our stories, we talk about our parents, siblings, childhood experiences, nuclear and extended family members, the schools we attended, our career and livelihood, our workplaces, ordination to the priesthood, religious profession, marriage, children, important events in our lives, people we have loved and those who have loved us, as well as agonies, death, and other losses we have incurred.

Because stories define our identity and selfhood, when there is loss of memory through age, cerebral accident, Alzheimer's, dementia, or any other illness that causes brain damage, we no longer know who we are, and we cannot tell our stories. Certainly, our stories reflect our truth since human beings cannot function properly without a narrative of identity – stories like when and where we were born, who our parents are, our developmental history, etc. Schreiter calls these true stories or narratives of identity, orthodoxies – our right ways of believing.[6] These stories tell us how we are introduced to religion, God, moral life, and cultural values, how we have changed or not changed, how we have matured or not, how we have remembered what happened to us, the love we have received or not received from

---

[6] Schreiter, 1992, 37.

parents and siblings, and how we have managed to be who we are. Indeed, these stories can change with time and are told differently or are modified from time to time by violence.

Schreiter defines violence as "an attack on our sense of safety and selfhood."[7] In other words, violence is an attack on our story, which is our true identity and selfhood. A violent attack, such as physical violence, emotional, economic, or sexual abuse, affects a person's sense of safety because the person is treated not with dignity but with contempt or as a lump of trash in a bin. When the true narrative is attacked, it results in a false story, which Schreiter calls the "narrative of the lie" or heterodoxy (another way of believing).[8] The reason for this term is that our orthopraxis has been countered by another way of believing since violence negates our true story and provides another narration so that the victim will learn to adhere to the will of the abuser. He explains that this attack on our identity reminds us of our vulnerability and can lead to doubting or abandoning the true story that defines our identity.[9]

Quoting Lenore Walker, a psychologist, Rita-Lou Clarke calls this vulnerable life of an abused woman learned helplessness."[10] Clarke explains that when a woman is repeatedly abused, she believes that she cannot control the situation any longer. Thus, she becomes helpless and responds passively and submissively to her situation. Clarke continues that this helpless state can persist until an external force intervenes. As a result of this learned helplessness,

---

[7] Ibid.
[8] Ibid, 34, 37.
[9] Ibid, 34.
[10] Clarke, 36-37.

many women remain in abusive relationships not because they like to be beaten, but because they are helpless, economically dependent, and because they do not have a safe place to go. Consequently, most abused women suffer depression, great fear and anxiety, low self-esteem, miscarriage, physical injury, death, diseases, unwanted pregnancies, drug addiction, suicide, loss of confidence, and lack of trust. Schreiter notes that this state of affairs reminds us how fragile our stories are and that they can be interrupted at any time. This false narrative is used to maintain violence since it will finally be accepted as the truth when the original story is completely suppressed. And any attempt on the part of the victim to resurrect the true story is always met with more violence. For this reason, some women in abusive relationships decide to keep quiet, accept that they are no good, and suffer violent behavior silently.

Some wounded women do not remain silent for long. They desire to regain their identity, true story, and dignity. Most of the time, assistance comes from the outside so that the victim of abuse can learn ways to redeem her identity. When an abused woman realizes the power and choices she has, her strength grows, and her helplessness fades.[11] However, a victim of abuse begins the journey of redeeming her distorted stories and identity through a reconciliation process. According to Schreiter, these are the steps of this process: first, acknowledging that damage has been done in replacing one's story with a false story; second, crying and lamenting over it rather than bearing the oppression in silence; and third, finding another

---

[11] Clarke, 40.

narrative to replace the false story.[12] For Schreiter, crying out or lamenting names the abuser, gives voice to the pain, and calls others to the side of the victim. Lamenting over her lost identity is also an appeal to God. On the other hand, silence is the friend of the oppressor.[13] By breaking the cycle of abuse through lamenting and naming the immoral act, the victim begins to gain control over the violent behavior and is ready to recover and embrace a new identity.

However, the new story will never be the same because it is somewhat associated with violence. Nonetheless, a new story is needed for the victim to be relieved from her trauma and damaged memory. Schreiter calls this new narrative orthopathema – the right way to suffer.[14]

When the orthodoxy (the right way of believing) is replaced with violence or the narrative of a lie (heterodoxy), then the victim needs to regain her humanity and respect through orthopathema. However, the regaining of the victim's humanity and respect has to come from the victim through her crying out for help. And since the victim could regain her identity through overt lamenting, any attempt by the victim to go public is often met with threats of more violence by the abuser. Thus, the relationship between violence and reconciliation is that reconciliation confronts the violence, removes or uproots the grip violence has on its victim, and helps the victim regain her humanity. The process of reconciliation brings healing to the victim and rebuilds the damage that the false narrative has had on the

---

[12] Schreiter, 1992, 36-37.

[13] Ibid., 37.

[14] Ibid. (The term "orthopathema" was introduced to Schreiter by Samuel Solivan, a Hispanic theologian).

victim's self-esteem. This process takes time; however, it redeems the victim and replaces the imposed false story with a new narrative.

I will use the story of Adaugo, a Nigerian woman, to demonstrate how a true story changes. She is an educated, wealthy, and beautiful young lady who has been married for ten years. At the start of their marriage, her husband adored and cherished her, showering her with precious gifts. He even affectionately called Adaugo "Obidiya," which means "the heart of the husband." Adaugo also had a pet name for her husband, "Obim" (My Heart). Their first child was a girl whom they adored and treated like royalty. Their relationship changed after the birth of their second baby girl. The husband had hoped for a boy. The husband's first sign of distance was dropping the pet name Obidiya and addressing her by her real name, "Adaugo."

The situation worsened when the third child also turned out to be a girl. Adaugo's husband became very aggressive. He frequently returned home late and started battering his wife. He abused her sexually, physically, and emotionally. Adaugo often attended community gatherings with swollen eyes or face, but no one noticed her predicament because she concealed it with a smiling face. Several times, the husband asked Adaugo: "What do you think I am going to do with these daughters of yours? You are no good if you cannot give me a son. Why did I ever marry a beautiful witch who eats the sons she conceived?" He referred to his daughters as "ama ndi ozo" (meaning that his daughters would have a new home after they got married). He persistently used verbal attacks to demand his wife for a son to continue his lineage. This behavior continued for several years, and Adaugo suffered in silence and was passive to this abuse. She blamed herself for her predicament and wondered why God refused to give her a son. She even claimed that her sins were the cause of her cross and perceived herself as worthless. Because her husband threatened divorce if anyone should learn of his abusive manners, Adaugo isolated herself from all her friends and family members.

After a thorough beating by her husband one night, Adaugo ran away from their home on a Sunday morning. She took shelter with her family members and vowed never to go back to her husband, and with the help of her family members, she filed for a divorce. The husband was taken aback. He never knew that Adaugo could be that brave. He destroyed his peaceful home, and the consequences of his actions were staring him in the face. "A rainmaker who invokes rain on his people cannot prevent rain from his own compound," says an African proverb. Adaugo's husband has brought home "a firewood infested with ants; the lizards are unceremoniously invited." He was utterly confused and began to seek peace and reconciliation at any cost. He even sought advice from their pastor to help him persuade Adaugo to return home. But all his pleading fell on deaf ears. The pastor implored Adaugo to let go of the past, forgive her husband, and return home, but Adaugo chose to stay at her parent's home. As time passed, both Adaugo and her husband began attending counseling sessions with a psychologist, albeit at different times, until they were ready to undergo the reconciliation process together. Adaugo and her husband worked hard to rebuild and revive their failing marriage. After two years, Adaugo managed to heal and began to see herself as worthy of respect. As they worked toward reconciliation, both of them came to understand that both male and female children are blessings from God, and that the absence of a male child is not a result of any sin or the fault of the woman.

Before Adaugo got married, her story was one of dignity and respect. These attributes were part of her orthodoxy or her true story. She had a pet name and was showered with gifts. The story was changed to heterodoxy when a male child was not forthcoming, and Adaugo experienced domestic violence. She was called a witch, a good-for-nothing woman. She was blamed for the lack of a male child and threatened with divorce. Then something happened in her life. Adaugo became brave and did not keep quiet. She not only cried out for help, but she also filed for a divorce. She was aware of the effects of the abuse on her selfhood, her identity, and her body. She broke the violence with these words: "I cannot accept this abuse anymore. I deserve to be loved, respected, and treated as human. I need to live a fulfilled life free from oppression." With this awareness of self-worth, her new story (orthopathema) emerged, and the process of reconciliation, liberation, and peaceful co-existence started.

Clearly, this new narrative – orthopathema – will bear the scars of trauma. However, the new narrative helped Adaugo to begin the process of trusting again and restoring her dignity, which was distorted by the acts of violence. But what makes authentic reconciliation possible? What resources are available to the Church to become more involved in the reconciliation process? Authentic reconciliation is possible when the clergy and the community of the faithful understand what reconciliation is and what it is not.

Robert Schreiter identifies three models of reconciliation that are ineffective in the reconciliation process; they are: reconciliation as a hasty peace, reconciliation instead of liberation, and reconciliation as a managed process. These unproductive forms of the reconciliation process will be explained below. Although the grace of reconciliation is God's gift, understanding why these reconciliation processes are not very helpful may aid the pastors and pastoral workers to become effective ministers of reconciliation so that the healing of the victim of abuse can gradually take place.

The Ineffective Methods of the Reconciliation Process

For reconciliation to take place, it must be accompanied by truth. The process of restoring a wounded relationship is not always easy. It requires time, patience, sacrifice, humility, the ability to let go and forgive, as well as sincere love. It also requires empathic listening without judgment, arrogance, or false pride. When reflecting on these positive qualities that this process requires, I recalled the story of the two wolves in human beings:

> One evening, an old Cherokee told his grandson about the battle that goes on inside people. He said, "My son, the battle is between two wolves. One is evil, and it comes with anger, greed, arrogance, self-pity, guilt, resentment, inferiority, lies, and false pride. The other is good, and it comes with joy, peace, love, serenity, humility, kindness, empathy, benevolence, truth, compassion, forgiveness, and faith." The grandson thought about these wolves for a minute and asked his

grandfather, "Which wolf wins?" The old man responded: "The one you feed."[15]

This parable could be compared with the struggle of St. Paul when he described the war in his members. St. Paul explained: "For I do not do the good I want, but the evil I do not want is what I do.... So, I find it to be a law that when I want to do right, evil lies close at hand. For I delight in the law of God in my inmost self, but I see in my members another law at war with the law of my mind and making me captive to the law of sin which dwells in my members" (Romans 7:15-25).

Human wounds are not healed by becoming captive to the law of sin or with the trait of the evil wolf, but rather with the attribute of the good one. Unfortunately, we are sometimes inclined to feed the evil wolves in us, which destroy and complicate our relationship with one another. When a relationship is broken, we desire and seek to reconcile and settle our differences with one another, but we sometimes follow a makeshift process in order to fix things. The process of our reconciliation with God after the Fall will be a good example of an authentic way of going about the reconciliation journey.

After the Fall, the relationship between human beings and God was broken. It costs the life of Jesus on the cross in order to amend our broken relationship with God. The Scripture tells us that Christ reconciled us to God when we were yet sinners (Romans 5:10; 2 Corinthians 5:18; Colossians 1:20-21). The fact that we needed reconciliation means that our relationship with God was broken. Since

---

[15] Gupte, 26.

God is holy, our sins alienated us from Him. Thus, the result of Jesus' sacrifice is that our relationship with God was restored, we become heirs and friends of God rather than enemies: "I no longer call you servants…, but I call you friends" (John. 15:15). On the other hand, reconciliation in a Christian perspective does not have to be on the cross, but it calls for sacrifice, forgiveness, empathy, compassion, and love. It can take different forms and methods; some are not helpful while others are fruitful and efficient.

Reconciliation as a Hasty Peace

According to Robert Schreiter, reconciliation is not a hasty peace. This is a situation where reconciliation is attempted without getting to the root of the problem. Here, the memory of the brutality is suppressed, and the history of the hostility is put behind in order to let bygones be bygones. When memories of violence are overlooked, the reconciler is actually continuing the oppression because the root of the problem is not uncovered or confronted. By implication, the reconciler is suggesting that the experience of the abused woman is unimportant to the process. Schreiter states that "to trivialize and ignore memory is to trivialize and ignore human dignity and identity."[16] Of course, we all long for peace and tranquility in our families. However, when we hurry the reconciliation process in order to attain peace at all costs, we let the sleeping dog lie, yet the wounds the cruel manners of the partner inflicted on the victim of abuse are ignored and disregarded.

---

[16] Schreiter, 1992, 19.

Similarly, in the bid to mend broken relationships and achieve harmony, we fear breaking open the supposed "healed wound." One hears comments like, "Let us leave the past memories behind and face the bright future with hope." Inasmuch as it is not healthy to dwell in the past, it is equally very unhelpful for the victims of abuse not to retell their stories, especially to the hearing of the perpetrators of abuse. When these stories are told over and over again in bitterness, the experience relieves the burden the victims of abuse are carrying. Because reconciliation as a hasty peace belittles the memory of the abused woman as insignificant, this model is indeed the opposite of the reconciliation process, which values memories.

Schreiter continues that some Church leaders are guilty of this kind of reconciliation model. In the bid to follow the "Christian tradition of reconciliation, they stress correctly the theme of Christian forgiveness while ignoring the root source of the problem of violence." Adaugo, in our story above, experienced this hasty peace when her pastor counseled her to forget the past and forgive her husband, who was on his bended knees. Is it realistic and possible that Adaugo could forget the past hurt, hateful, detestable, despicable, abominable, repulsive, and malicious behavior of her husband? I do not doubt that getting to the root of the problem will make room for lasting peace, as evidenced by Adaugo's story.

Sometimes, the clerics are only concerned with the permanence of the sacrament of marriage by placing this institution over and above the integrity of the people in the sacramental union. This is comparable to when the Pharisees placed the Sabbath over and above the dignity of those seeking healing. However, Jesus challenged the Pharisees that the Sabbath is made for humankind and not humankind for the Sabbath (Mark 2:27). Rita-Lou Clarke notes that some pastors occasionally counsel an abused and wounded woman with various Bible verses: Jesus reminds us to forgive seventy-seven times (Matthew 18:22); to love our enemies and pray for those who persecute us (Matthew 5:44). Jesus also forgave those who crucified him: "Father forgive them; for they know not what they do" (Luke 23:34). Quoting these scriptural passages does not bring genuine reconciliation nor does it take away the brutality of domestic abuse, especially when the foundation of the problem is not discovered and uprooted.

In line with Schreiter's view, Rita-Lou Clarke explains that for a battered woman, forgiveness should not be rushed since she must reshape herself from the one who has been devalued to the one who has value in the sight of God. Forgiveness and reconciliation take time to process. When reconciliation is rushed, it becomes a hasty peace that postpones and covers up the enormity of what has been done, as well as shortens the process. Apparently, the abuser is the one who calls for this kind of reconciliation process most of the time, probably after seeing the consequences of his actions.

When the hasty peace process is used, it does not take long before the abuser hurts his victim again. Schreiter believes that this process of reconciliation is driven by the fear that remembering past violence may lead to the eruption of new hostilities. This is a misunderstanding of the process of reconciliation because uncovering the history of abuse in a family is the fundamental repair to the lives of those who have suffered from violence. This fundamental repair began in the life of Adaugo when the root cause of the abuse was discovered and confronted. Her memory of the abuse was not suppressed. She did not surrender to the counseling of "forgetting the past and forgiving her husband." Actually, sharing her painful story brought healing to her and held her husband accountable for his cruel behavior. Adaugo gradually experienced healing through the reconciliation process and was able to forgive her husband at the proper time. Surely, allowing a victim of violence to share her experience is the beginning of healing and forgiveness; on the other hand, suppressing the story belittles the gravity of the offense. Thus, reconciliation can only occur when the nature, memory, and root cause of violence are acknowledged, and the conditions for its continuation are avoided.

Reconciliation Instead of Liberation

The second dynamic of an ineffective reconciliation process is "when liberation is seen as an alternative to reconciliation rather than its prerequisite."[17] Because liberation is the act of releasing a person from oppression into freedom, it has to take place before true reconciliation can be achieved. Schreiter explains that we call for liberation in order to bring about reconciliation, for without liberation, there will be no reconciliation. When Christians engage in liberation in order to bring about reconciliation, it is a process in the right direction since genuine reconciliation can only take place when the structures and processes that permit and promote violence are dismantled. On the other hand, engaging in the reconciliation process as an alternative to liberation does not acknowledge the deep reali-

---

[17] Schreiter, 1992, 79.

ties of the wound of abuse; it assumes that violence can be speedily and easily overcome.

I will use Adaugo's story to illustrate the point further. During the two years of attempting to reconcile, Adaugo's husband identified the root cause of their problems: his extramarital affair. Their problem was not necessarily caused by having only female children. The husband admitted to being unfaithful to his wife, and this extramarital relationship was putting strain on their family. By acknowledging and denouncing the hidden issue as a betrayal, and terminating the unfaithful relationship, the family was able to reunite, albeit with difficulty in rebuilding their trust. The process of liberation was necessary for healing and authentic reconciliation to occur. This involved naming, examining, and condemning the source of the conflict before commencing true reconciliation between them.

The theology of liberation is very much needed in African society. Some African traditions are very oppressive, yet people are reluctant to change. This reluctance to change can be illustrated by the experience of Rose Uchem, a religious sister, during her visit to the home of one of her religious sisters. Uchem was given a kola nut to bless and break in the presence of men.[18] As chapter one explains, the kola nut ritual is the prayer for thanksgiving, peace, blessing, protection, and goodwill that unites the living and the dead. In Igbo culture, it is unacceptable for a woman to bless, break, and share a kola nut before men. Uchem was given this honor, perhaps because she was a religious sister or because some men from that part of Igbo culture are coming to the realization that prayer and blessing can be

---

[18] Uchem, 239.

Chapter 3: Toward a Genuine Reconciliation Process 89

reciprocal. However, Uchem did not finish the ritual of blessing, breaking, and sharing the kola nut. She actually blessed the kola nut and passed the plate back to the man of the house to break and share it. Uchem inquired: "What dynamic internalized subordination held me back from breaking the kola nut I had been graciously offered?" Her response was that perhaps it was taboo for women to break the kola nut before men. Or maybe it was a matter of courtesy and respect for the owner of the house. Genuine liberation of women will take place only when women see themselves as equal partners with men. Evidently, there is a need to abolish repressive and exploitative structures in African society so that transformation can prevail.

Schreiter suggests that the Church falls prey to this second model of reconciliation not as a direct violator but because the Church maintains silence in the face of oppressive culture.[19] In other words, the Church participates in the violation of the victims of abuse because the Church leaders often fear to go deeper into the root cause of abuse. Take, for instance, the widowhood ritual in Nigeria. This ritual is practiced by some Christians (the story of Lady Regina Igwemezie used above is a good example), but how many priests can boldly condemn this practice as evil? How many priests can also courageously preach against the evils of domestic abuse that have eaten deep into the fabric of our society? A Zambian proverb explains that to "protect an individual is to protect society."[20] If family values are not upheld, then society will suffer the effects of having a broken

---

[19] Schreiter, 1992, 23.

[20] Annetta Miller, *African Wisdom on Leadership* (Nairobi, Kenya: Paulines Publications Africa, 2006).

community, and the Church will be affected, too, since the family is the domestic church.

Sometimes, when some priests start the reconciliation process, they emphasize the harmonious existence of conflicting interests rather than vehemently condemning oppressive traditions. However, genuine reconciliation and liberation must squarely meet and face conflict and its causes rather than appealing only to a harmonious existence. The Church, working through its pastors, must try to discover, uproot, and condemn the root source of violence against women and admonish abusers to desist from sinful action. Moreover, peaceful existence can only occur when the spiritual, social, political, and cultural structures that perpetuate violence fall apart, resulting in the authentic liberation that is a necessary precondition for genuine reconciliation.

Reconciliation as a Managed Process

The final model for an ineffective reconciliation process is when reconciliation is managed as a disciplined process, i.e., when "both parties get to accept and live with their conflictual situation through a bargaining process."[21] This process calls the spouses to a harmonious relationship through a give-and-take method. Here, a skilled mediator helps the spouses recognize the issues at stake so that a balancing process can be undertaken to achieve reconciliation. This kind of reconciliation acknowledges that both parties have legitimate interests, and both are expected to relinquish some of their interests

---

[21] Ibid.

to accommodate each other before the conflict can be resolved. In other words, each party (the oppressor and the victim) has interests, dignity, and values that must be acknowledged, and acting contrary to them may bring the parties at odds with each other. Schreiter states that this reconciliation process "falls short of the Christian understanding of reconciliation because it reduces reconciliation to a technical rationality or a skill that can be taught in order to deal with a problem."[22]

But for Christians, reconciliation is what God does. God awakens in the victim and, likewise, in the oppressor the need to seek reconciliation and heart conversion. Ultimately, surrendering some interests cannot nip the problem in the bud. Some interests are still retained, and they could be the source of the problem that has to be uprooted and named. The story below will illustrate clearly what reconciliation as a managed process entails.

In Kenya, Murimi and his wife Faraji were happily married and gainfully employed. After five years of marriage, Murimi began complaining that Faraji didn't have enough time for their relationship due to her busy office schedule. He asked Faraji to resign from her job and promised to take care of their household's financial burdens. When Faraji refused to quit her job, Murimi became aggressive and violent. He physically abused his wife due to trivial reasons such as burnt food, a messy house, and a delayed meal. Faraji could not tolerate Murimi's battering anymore; she reported her husband's violent activities to their parish priest. When they both met with the pastor, Murimi insisted that Faraji must let go of her job for peace to reign

---

[22] Ibid., 26.

in their relationship. The pastor encouraged Faraji to listen to her husband, as he was the head of the family and had promised to take care of their financial needs.

After much bargaining, the "expected peace" was attained when Faraji quit her job and became a full-time housewife. Unfortunately, no one cared about the effects of abuse on Faraji or the consequences of the relinquished job. She had to obey the societal structures and her husband as expected. However, the peace achieved through a negotiation process did not last. They divorced within six months of this incident because the family's financial needs were not adequately met, and Faraji was unhappy being a full-time housewife. Murimi did not remember the African proverb that suggests that being a leader is like a borrowed garment. It can be reclaimed at any time by the owner.

Faraji is now a happily married woman with two children, and her job is to help sustain the new family. However, Faraji had to undergo the reconciliation process to regain this happiness. During this process, she was able to let go and mourn the dead relationship with Murimi, forgive her ex-husband even though their relationship was never restored, and finally find joy in regaining her dignity as a woman. Today, Fariji can say, "Although I am a happy woman, I still remember what I went through with Murimi. However, I recall it not with sadness, but with a peaceful and forgiving spirit."

From the explanations above and all indications, we have observed that these models of reconciliation (reconciliation as a hasty peace, reconciliation instead of liberation, and reconciliation as a managed process) are insufficient methods in the reconciliation process. This is because rushing through the process of reconciliation for the sake of a hasty peace overlooks the underlying issue and requires an improvised approach by suppressing the memories of the victims. Another fact is that liberation is a prerequisite for reconciliation. Until the structures that enable discrimination and violence are eradicated, true reconciliation cannot occur, and gender equality will not be achieved. The final model – reconciliation as a managed process – does not hold the abuser accountable because both the abuser and his victim are expected to use a bargaining process in order to settle their problems. However, the abuser is always responsible for his acts of violence since he could use other options to communicate his anger than violent behavior. Below is the genuine reconciliation process that can help victims of abuse deal with the damage and the false narrative acquired through domestic violence.

The Process of True Reconciliation

Inasmuch as we continue to stress that reconciliation is what God does, we are also to be aware that the victim of abuse has a part to play. As explained above, violence damages the self-identity of a woman and renders her helpless, passive, and believing a false narrative of her abuser. Genuine reconciliation, on the other hand, addresses violence, eliminates the hold violence has on the victim, and assists the victim in reclaiming her humanity and her true narrative. The process of true reconciliation requires using the right people, the right approach, and the right timing in order for it to be effective.

Using the Right People

Each human person is gifted differently, but not everyone is gifted with the skills to reconcile the victims of abuse. Thus, genuine reconciliation requires the right people. What we are advocating here is not necessarily those who are witty, clever, and can negotiate tactfully, discreetly, and convincingly; although, these traits are important. However, when this personality is used, it may sometimes lead to reconciliation as a managed process where bargaining is used to persuade the victim to accept the outcome of the process. The use of the right people in a true and effective reconciliation process is usually in the form of a support group.

This group should be a safe place where victims explore their wounds and hurt, where redemptive memories are recovered, where the truth is told, and where justice is done.[23] Because women are usually the victims of domestic violence, they are also the ones who survive and teach others how to cope and move on; thus, this support group should only be for women who have an interest in empowering victims of violence. Schreiter explains that women are "the ambassadors of reconciliation par excellence, and they find a non-violent way out of violent situations."[24] In other words, women are often left to find ways of repairing the damage that men's violence has wrought on their humanity.

---

[23] Robert Schreiter, *The Ministry of Reconciliation: Spirituality and Strategies* (Maryknoll, NY: Orbis Books, 1998), 94-95.

[24] Schreiter, 1998, 94.

Because a wounded woman is likely to seek help first from the parish pastor, it is important for parishes to have a support group for such circumstances. Seeking help is the first step in the reconciliation process. It shows that the victim of abuse is aware of the need to embrace a new story and relinquish the burden of anger, bitterness, pain, and trauma that are caused by domestic violence. Therefore, every pastor probably needs to find a woman trained in counseling and psychology skills as well as one who has experience or training in domestic violence to lead the support group. However, the pastor must work hand in hand with the group by providing pastoral care, supporting each victim, and getting information on their progress. This support group will be open to every wounded woman in need of healing. Each pastor has to announce through the parish bulletins or verbally during liturgy the goal of the group and how it will help women who are suffering to regain their humanity. Another way the pastor can create awareness of this group is to allow the woman leader to speak about the group and its goal to all the parish's women. The women who are wounded may find ways to become members.

Using the Right Approach

When members of the group are formed, empathic listening and confidentiality must be the group's guiding principle in the process of reconciliation. However, much time will be needed to create an atmosphere of trust and a safe space before the process can efficiently begin. According to Schreiter, "the victims of violence must tell their stories over and over again in order to escape the narratives of the lie. And as they recount these stories, little by little they begin to construct new narratives of truth that include the experiences of suffering and violence which may no longer be overwhelming."[25] Because the group's stories are repeated, they should be available and willing to listen as each member recounts her story. Consequently, new narratives will emerge because the abused has realized that she is valued, respected, loved, and supported by the group members. Schreiter asks how long or how often a story must be retold before it turns into a redemptive story rather than an oppressive one.[26] He acknowledges that no one can ever know for sure since the moment or grace of reconciliation comes to the victim as a surprise. At this stage, the ministry of the leader of the group is to listen empathically in a non-judgmental way, to accompany the victims, and not to minimize the abuse, give instructions, or blame the victims. Schreiter uses the story of the Stranger and the two disciples walking to Emmaus (Luke. 24:13-35) to demonstrate how hope can be regained through telling a story.[27]

On their way to Emmaus, the two disciples were disheartened, disappointed, and disillusioned; "We had hoped that he would save Israel" (Lk. 24:21). The Stranger joined them and gently gained their trust and provided a safe place for them to tell their story. As they journeyed along the road, the Stranger compassionately listened to them, retold their story, and accompanied them gradually. Schreiter notes that "the story retold begins to restore their humanity: they were able to offer hospitality to the Stranger." The moment they

---

[25] Schreiter, 1992, 71.
[26] Schreiter, 1998, 46.
[27] Ibid.

recognized Jesus was a moment of grace, of reconciliation, of transformation, and of new hope and joy. Empathic listening and creating a safe place to revisit memories and reveal wounds are essential for the support group. This kind of non-judgmental listening helps the abused to discover and confront the problem of abuse that she is facing. Consequently, the victim feels heard, respected, and valued.

To attract more women to the support group, the pastor can invite speakers from time to time to give several seminars on: the realities and domination of patriarchal culture, the consequences of domestic abuse, the empowerment of women who are wounded, Jesus' care for women, the equality of the human person, the reflections on John Paul II's documents, e.g., on *"The Theology of the Body," "Letter to Women," "Familiaris consortio," "Gratissimam sane,"* etc. Education is power. Enlightenment seminars can empower women to reject outdated cultural traditions.

When I was working with the twelve ladies I mentioned above, the support group was very helpful as it provided a safe space for the women to share their stories and engage in the process of reconciliation. They were comfortable with being vulnerable. However, it took time to build trust and confidence in the group, and confidentiality was crucial. Because these women were grieving for almost the same experience, they were inspired and encouraged to go through the process. They felt heard, and the group provided them with a great opportunity to release their burden and pain.

This support group could meet weekly or bi-weekly to share their stories and monitor the progress of their healing process. The leader of the group and the pastor must also create spaces of safety for abused women, especially those who may be reluctant to spread all their "dirty rags" in public. Because sharing abusive incidents can be embarrassing, the pastor or the leader can have one-on-one counseling with the abused woman. For this reason, every pastor needs training in domestic abuse and counseling to understand available resources and offer appropriate help in different abuse cases.

The second step to the right approach is to continue to confront the effect of the abuse in a more personal way. Louise Hay, an American motivational author, suggested many creative processes of releasing emotions, such as screaming into a pillow, kicking the pillow, beating or punching a bag, writing a letter, and burning it.[28] The ability to confront and address violence helps abuse victims begin releasing the burden of abuse.

The Process of Releasing the Pain of Abuse

- Find a comfortable and sacred space where you will be alone
- Bring an object (e.g., a pillow) that represents the perpetrator of the violence in front of you.
- Prayerfully but sternly speak to it as you would talk with an opponent.
- Tell the object your whole story, how it all started, and where you are at the moment.
- Tell it how you feel and how it has messed up your true narrative.

---

[28] Louise Hay, *The Power is Within You* (Los Angele, CA: Hay House, Inc., 1991).

Chapter 3: Toward a Genuine Reconciliation Process

- Tell the personified object that you are reclaiming your dignity as a woman.
- If you feel like beating the object as you would beat the abuser, do it.
- While going through the process, allow yourself to cry, if you feel the need to, and express your emotions out loud by naming them.
- After the process, stay calm and pray with the experience
- Do some journaling: Honestly, express in writing the pain, harm, injury, hurt, and the bitterness that you feel within. This is a way to pour out all the bottled feelings.
- If you are able, pray for the abuser and forgive him; if not, hand him over to God. God will bring you to forgiveness at the right time.
- The result of this process of confrontation and journaling is the act of releasing and liberating oneself from the pain of abuse.

Some psychologists have found this method of letting out pain unproductive because they think that it keeps anger alive rather than erasing it.[29] Thomas Bellows, a psychologist, explains: "If we hit a pillow, we may feel better immediately after discharging our anger. Unfortunately, we are not constructively dealing with anger; we are

---

[29] Tim Murphy and Loriann Oberlin, *Overcoming Passive-Aggression: How to Stop Hidden Anger from Spoiling your Relationships, Career and Happiness* (Cambridge, MA: Da Capo Press, 2005), 33.

simply rehearsing aggressive behaviors."[30] In my experience of working with the victims of abuse, I found this method very helpful and productive, especially when the person using this process has already begun the journey of reconciliation. However, it can be counterproductive when the victim of abuse is only using it to release anger and aggression and she has not commenced the journey of reconciliation. Louise Hay further commented that if one cannot forgive after this exercise, then it is not healing for the person.

Letting-go is the third step in the right approach to the reconciliation process. It comes about when the victim of abuse has confronted the abuse and she is willing to embrace a new story. Letting go does not take the past experience away because the past is still part of who we are; however, it gives peace and joy to the victims as they remember the abuse in a new and different way. It leads to wholeness healing of the victim of abuse and gives her the grace to forgive the abuser and to reconcile with herself, God, and the community.

Embracing the new story is the last step in the right approach to the reconciliation journey. Because the true story of the victim of abuse is distorted, letting go of this distorted story, bitterness, anger, pain, resentment, and the trauma of abuse must pave the way for healing to take place and for the victim of abuse to seek an alternative story – *orthopathema*. Embracing the new narrative helps the victim to accept the past experiences and remember them differently. The victim prepares to forgive but will never forget.

---

[30] Thomas Bellows, *Happiness in the Family: Using Choice Theory to Eliminate Hostility in the Family* (Lincoln, NE: iUniverse Inc, 2007), 27.

Right Timing

Reconciliation that leads to healing is a process that takes time. Certainly, it takes time for the victims of abuse to grieve, cry, and express all that has happened in order for them to let go of hurtful experiences, anger, pain, and trauma caused by domestic violence. A saying goes that only time can heal a broken heart or wound. This saying will be possible when the victim of abuse and the abuser, if possible, desire to go through the process of reconciliation gradually without rushing to fix things, as it is the case of reconciliation through hasty peace. Schreiter concurs that learning to wait is important to the process of reconciliation.[31] Sometimes, we are in a hurry to fix things. We consider waiting as a waste of time. Although delay can be dangerous, especially where the life of the woman is at risk, waiting may also serve a good purpose. Waiting is important because healing takes time; painful memories and experiences also take time to be retold. It is waiting on God and God's reconciling grace.

For Schreiter, learning to wait involves being calm and comfortable with ourselves, which is something the victims of violence must relearn. Indeed, this waiting is not an empty time that should elapse before things happen. Rather, it is part of the healing process that moves the victim from illusion into reality, from the stories of the lie to the narrative of the truth. Waiting also can help the victims of abuse to pay great attention to God and the condition of torture, fear, and mistrust that surround their experiences.

---

[31] Schreiter, 1992, 71.

This fear and mistrust are sometimes created by the power imbalance in families. To minimize this imbalance of power, the Christian women, men, and youth in Christian communities must internalize the values of equality for every human person. To achieve this value, the pastors can organize several workshops for diverse groups of married men and women, single adults, and youth groups. Speakers can be invited during each workshop for a different group to raise the issues concerning conflict resolution without violence, effects of male superior culture on women, domestic abuse and its consequences, theology of justice, freedom, and fairness, authentic parenting, gender issues, equality of all, feelings and the inappropriate expression, empowerment of women, and non-violent behavior/communication.

The values of the workshops will be the awareness of the evils of male domination and the effects of violence on women. The goal is to propose alternative ways of responding to anger, internalization of the equality of males and females, reciprocity in parental roles, non-violent communication, peaceful co-existence, mutual interdependence, and mutual love. Thus, Christian women will be enlightened and empowered to organize themselves and reject any tradition at home or in society that is oppressive to them. As a result of all these seminars and workshops, an abused woman will no longer perceive marriage as a parcel, and whatever she finds inside it must be embraced. Rather, she may regard marriage as an equal union of a man and a woman united in God's love.

It is equally advisable for clergymen to refer the abused woman to where she can find help if he is not competent in handling domestic abuse cases and if the parishioners cannot find an adequate leader for the support group. This means that each parish must have the phone numbers and the physical addresses of non-governmental organizations and safety homes caring for battered women. However, each priest can begin pastoral care with the basic step of empathic listening and follow up on the woman's progress after referring her to a safe home or an NGO that cares for abused women.

This chapter has tried to explain genuine reconciliation and the relationship between violence and reconciliation. It also illustrated that some methods in the reconciliation process may not be helpful. It goes on to demonstrate and propose the true reconciliation process that will be helpful for women who are abused, that is, using the right people, the right approach, and the right timing. Although reconciliation and healing are gifts from God, each victim of abuse undergoes the process of reconciliation and healing uniquely and at a different pace. However, the victims of abuse and possibly the abuser have to realize that abuse is sinful and for the victim to work towards restoring her distorted story. How does the abused person realize a false story imposed on her? In other words, what role can the Church communities play in the healing process of the battered woman to enable her to embrace a new story? The next chapter will explain the genuine healing that takes place through the process of reconciliation: physical, spiritual, and emotional. It will clarify the role of the church in the healing process, the healing message of the gospel, and how forgiveness aids in the healing process. It will also elaborate on the power of ritual in the healing process so that a redemptive story will emerge.

Chapter 4

Genuine Healing through the Process of Reconciliation

"For Christians, a resort to violence reveals a failure to trust in God and God's purposes in every human situation."

—*Gaudium et Spes*, no. 79

The reconciliation process must occur with some necessary conditions. As explained in chapter three, when God's grace awakens in the victim of abuse the need to seek reconciliation, this consciousness confronts violent behavior and the narrative of the lie and brings about healing. Although God initiates reconciliation, the victim of violence must begin the process of reconciliation through the experience of grace.[1] The experience of grace is thus the experience of reconciliation. This reminds me of a parable of two frogs:

> Once upon a time, two frogs were hopping along together when they had the misfortune of jumping into a bucket of milk. They swarm for hours and hours hoping to get out somehow, but in vain. After some struggling, one of the frogs gave up hope and was drowned. The other frog decided to keep on paddling. He thought: "Where there is life, there is

---

[1] Schreiter, 1992, 43.

hope." The frog kept on swimming round and round the bucket, and this movement formed the milk into white waves. After a while, just as he felt completely numb and thought he was about to drown, he suddenly felt something solid and that he was resting on a lump of butter which was churned up by constant paddling. And so, the successful frog leaped out of the bucket of milk to freedom.[2]

The successful frog was alive because of its will to arise and determination to live again. When the power to survive dies in a human person, there will be no hope of seeking transformation, liberation, reconciliation, and healing. Therefore, the victims of violence must choose healing and liberation by cooperating with the grace of God.

This chapter will illustrate how the Church, as the minister of the reconciliation process, can create an environment in its community that will move the victims of abuse to seek her true story that is distorted with lies. The goal of reconciliation is to facilitate healing and for the victim of violence to adopt a new narrative that contradicts the false narrative. Therefore, this chapter will also explain what healing is – physical, spiritual, and emotional. It will clarify what forgiveness does in the healing process, the grace and love of Jesus in the Gospel messages that can move the victim of violence to seek reconciliation which results in healing, and the power of ritual in the healing process. Similarly, the abuser is also in need of conversion, forgiveness, and healing. The Word of God can help both the abuser

---

[2] Gupte, 15.

and the victim understand the impact of abuse on their relationship, how the victim's story has changed, and the mercy of God in her life.

One might wonder why the process of healing through reconciliation has to start with the victim rather than the abuser's repentance of his wrongdoing. Schreiter clarifies that it is often difficult for the abuser to accept and acknowledge that what he has done is wrong. Thus, if reconciliation depends on him, then there might be no reconciliation.[3] Similarly, from my experience at the Home for Abused Women and Children, some abusers often show remorse and lavish their victims with love only to hurt them again and again. That God would begin the process of healing with the victim is in line with God's activity in the history of salvation. God takes the side of the poor, the orphans, and the oppressed. Therefore, it is through the victim of abuse that the abuser is called to repentance, forgiveness, and healing.[4]

Healing – Physical, Emotional, and Spiritual

The word healing is from the old English word of Germanic origin – hælan, and in German – heilen which means to restore to wholeness or sound health, to cure, save, or make well.[5] The etymology of healing suggests that when it takes place, one is drawn towards the awareness and the experience of wholeness – physical, emotional, and spiritual – encompassing body, mind, and spirit,

---

[3] Schreiter, 1998, 14.
[4] Schreiter, 1998, 15.
[5] Online Etymology Dictionary, www.etymonline.com/index.php?term=heal.

respectively. Genuine healing addresses these components with the goal of re-establishing a right relationship with self, God, and others. However, it is God who heals wholesomely through Jesus. "By his wounds, we are healed" (1 Peter 2:24; Isaiah 53:5). Healing, in this reflection, is the process of restoring to wholeness the physical, emotional, and spiritual wounds of the victims of violence. Although complete restoration may not take place, the victims need to be freed from the burdens of violence.

When there is domestic violence in a family, a woman can sustain a physical injury through battering, slapping, kicking, pushing, pulling of her hair, throwing of objects, using a weapon like a gun, knife, or any other sharp object to inflict injury, as well as other illnesses that are caused by traumatic experiences. For instance, losing an arm during violence could be very traumatic and painful. However, to wallow in self-pity over the lost arm will never change the situation of the individual. Like Morrie, in *Tuesdays with Morrie*,[6] the transformational thing to do is accept what cannot be changed, mourn the lost arm, and concentrate on the good things life offers.

Morrie Schwartz, an old professor of Mitch, was diagnosed with a terminal sickness – ALS (Amyotrophic Lateral Sclerosis). And because his illness was incurable, he decided to live with dignity, courage, composure, and humor. He said: "Do I wither up and disappear, or do I make the best of my time left?" (p. 10). Although on many occasions Morrie cried and asked whether it was fair to suffer in this manner, he was at the same time very cheerful and positive about death. He says, "When you learn how to die, you learn how to live"

---

[6] Mitch Albom, *Tuesdays with Morrie* (New York: Doubleday, 1997).

(p. 104). He was not afraid of shedding tears because that is how healing is attained: "Wash yourself with the emotion. It won't hurt you. It will only help you…. Let the tears flow, feel it completely" (p. 105). Morrie experienced healing even though there was no cure for his illness. While mourning the slow and insidious way in which he was dying, he concentrated on the good things of his life and his ability to say goodbye to people he loved (p. 57). Thus, while having no hope of physical wellness, he experienced emotional and spiritual healing.

Emotional healing is needed when there is psychological trauma or wounds caused by abuse in the form of name-calling, public humiliation, marital rape, stalking, intimidation, demeaning language, insulting words, sexual abuse, spreading false rumors, etc. The experiences of this abuse may cause insomnia, incessant headaches or backaches, nightmares, anger, depression, mood swings, self-blame, anxiety or fear, withdrawal from friends and relatives, confusion, shame, guilt, helplessness, etc. Emotional and spiritual healing are attained through the process of reconciliation, forgiveness, therapy sessions, and ultimately by God's grace.

Spiritual healing takes place when emotional healing is attained. Stuart Grayson, a pastor and philosopher, explained that for us to understand how spiritual healing happens, we must understand how our minds work. He continued that spiritual healing results from a change in our underlying consciousness and belief rather than from focusing on physical symptoms and manifestations as medical practitioners do.[7] In other words, when the negative energy of the state of helplessness of the victim of abuse is broken, and the root cause of the problem is dealt with, then spiritual healing, liberation, and forgiveness can gradually take place, and the victim of abuse will experience wholesome healing.

What Forgiveness Does in the Healing Process

This popular saying by Lewis Smedes in his book *Forgive and Forget: Healing the Hurts We Don't Deserve* is true about healing: "To forgive is to set a prisoner free and discover that the prisoner was you." Forgiveness leads to emotional and spiritual healing. Forgiveness does not necessarily lead to the restoration of a relationship because the victim of abuse can forgive the abuser but the relationship may be dead forever. In other words, there can be forgiveness without reconciliation. What forgiveness does is help the victim of abuse to give up resentment, hurt, trauma, and anger of the experiences of abuse and to remember it in a different and new way. It is not about denying them, but it is about letting go. Sometimes, we want to hold on to the hurt we are feeling, thereby imprisoning ourselves with more burden.

In *Tuesdays with Morrie*, Morrie explains: "Accept the past as past, without denying it or discarding it. Learn to forgive yourself and to forgive others. Don't assume that it is too late to get involved."[8]

---

[7] Stuart Grayson, *Spiritual Healing: A Simple Guide for the Healing of the Body, Mind and Spirit* (New York, NY: Simon & Schuster, 1997), 102.

[8] Albom, 18.

Actually, to forgive is to find within us a godlike goodness that asks for no return but only wishes for the good of the other.[9] It is a pure gift and unconditional. Indeed, forgiveness is what God does and it is an act of freedom and healing. For instance, Jesus did not forgive his executioners; he asked God to forgive them (Lk. 23:34). The Catechism of the Catholic Church explains: "Only God forgives sins. Since he is the Son of God, Jesus says of himself, "The Son of man has authority on earth to forgive sins" and exercises this divine power: "Your sins are forgiven" (Mk. 2:5; LK. 7:48).[10]

However, forgiveness is the most difficult part of the reconciliation process especially when the abuser does not acknowledge the violence as sin. That is why Mahatma Gandhi says: "Forgiveness is the attribute of the strong. The weak can never forgive." Forgiveness can be difficult also when it is seen as a betrayal of the past, a means to wipe out the memory of what has happened, or a pretense that all the pain never happened.[11] That is why the struggle to forgive has to come from the victim of abuse because the abuser might deny or minimize the gravity of the evil committed. Schreiter explains that we cannot forgive or pardon ourselves for our past wrongdoings since our consciences will haunt us until we have made amends with those we have wronged. Only those whom we have injured can forgive. For the battered woman, "forgiveness is going from a state of having the experience of being battered control her life to a whole

---

[9] Nicholas Ayo, *The Lord's Prayer: A Survey Theological and Literary* (Oxford, UK: Rowman & Littlefield Publishers, 2003), 76.

[10] CCC no. 1441.

[11] Robert Schreiter, *The Ministry of Reconciliation: Spirituality and Strategies*, 55.

new stance of being able to move on to a new experience."[12] The ability to forgive brings healing which restores the dignity and joy of the battered woman. Forgiveness is recognizing that the injured woman is human and has the dignity to be respected. It does not condone the act of abuse or excuse it; rather, forgiveness holds the abuser accountable.

When I think of emotional and spiritual healing, and the restoration of human dignity through forgiveness, the story that comes into my mind is the Parable of the Prodigal Son in Luke 15:11-32. Here the "Prodigal Father" extravagantly lavished his love, kind heart, compassion, and mercy on his wayward and reckless son. He did not count the loss he had sustained by his son's irresponsible and wasteful life; rather, he sought a genuine relationship with his son. As a result, the prodigal son was healed, and his human dignity was restored after he experienced a wayward life. Pope Francis has this to say during the midday angelus prayer with the audience on the 15th of September 2013 on forgiveness and the joy that emanates from a forgiving heart: "The joy of God is the joy of forgiveness. It is the joy of the shepherd who finds his lost sheep; the joy of the woman who finds her lost coin; the joy of the father who welcomes home his lost son."[13]

Another story of true forgiveness is the story of Joseph and his brothers in Genesis. The ten sons of Jacob conspired and sold Joseph, their brother. After many years, they thought Joseph was dead. When

---

[12] Clark, 79.

[13] Pope Francis, "Angelus: The Joy of God is the Joy of Forgiveness," News.Va: Official Vatican Network, September 15, 2013, www.news.va/en/news/angelus-the-joy-of-god-is-the- joy-of-forgiveness

they came to Egypt looking for food, they did not suspect that the man they were bowing to was their brother Joseph. When Joseph finally revealed himself to them, they were shocked to learn he was alive, and they all wept bitterly.

Even after this reconciliation, Joseph's brothers still feared that he had not forgiven them. Out of fear, they approached Joseph after Jacob's death, saying: "Your father gave this instruction before he died. 'Say to Joseph: I beg you, forgive the crime of your brothers and the wrong they did in harming you.' Therefore, please forgive the crime of the servants of the God of your father." When Joseph heard this, he wept bitterly again; his brothers also wept, fell down before him, and said, "We are here as your slaves." Joseph's response was the culmination of this story of forgiveness: "Do not be afraid! Am I in the place of God? Even though you intended to harm me, God intended it for good in order to preserve numerous people, as he is doing today. So have no fear; I will provide for you and your little ones." In this way, he reassured them, speaking kindly to them. (Genesis 50:15-21).

St. Pope John Paul II is another example when it comes to forgiving an enemy. On Wednesday, 13 May 1981, in St. Peter's Square in Vatican City, he was shot and wounded by Mehmet Ali Ağca while he was entering the square. The Pope was struck four times, and he suffered severe blood loss. Ağca was apprehended immediately and later sentenced to life in prison by an Italian court. Following the shooting, Pope John Paul II asked people: "Pray for my brother [Ağca] ... Whom I have sincerely forgiven." In 1983, he and Ağca met and spoke privately at the prison where Ağca was being held. Ağca reportedly kissed the Pope's ring at the conclusion of their visit. The

Pope was also in touch with Ağca's family over the years, meeting his mother in 1987.[14]

St. Pope John Paul II and Mehmet Ali Ağca during the prison visit

St. Pope John Paul II has this to say about forgiveness: "Certainly, forgiveness does not come spontaneously or naturally to people. Forgiving from the Heart can sometimes be heroic . . . Thanks to the healing power of love, even the most wounded heart can experience the liberating encounter with forgiveness."[15]

In the case of the victims of violence, forgiveness releases them from the clutches of trauma to the experiences of liberation, healing,

---

[14] Wikipedia, "Pope John Paul II Assassination Attempt," https://en.wikipedia.org/wiki/Pope_John_Paul_II_assassination_attempt

[15] Liz Kelly, May Crowing, Mass and Merton: And Other Reasons I Love Being Catholic (Chicago, IL: Loyola Press, 2006), 61.

and newness of life. Complete forgiveness occurs when the batterer has repented and confessed the sin rather than minimizing or denying the damage done to the victim. Sometimes, it is hard for the victims of abuse to forgive themselves. However, they need time to gradually go through the process of reconciliation, and at the right time, God will bring their hearts to forgive. However, the Church has a part to play in the healing and forgiving process.

The Role of the Church in the Healing Process

God initiates and carries the victim through the reconciliation process. However, God does this work through the Church and the victim's collaboration with the grace of God. The United States Catholic bishops suggest that the Church can help stop domestic abuse since "many abused women seek help first from the Church because they see it as a safe place." They continued: "Even if their abusers isolate them from other social contacts, they may still allow them to go to church."[16] Thus, through the gospel message and through the ministry of reconciliation, the Church provides redeeming narratives that may restore the truth and selfhood of an abused woman since the gift of this ministry is bestowed on the Church. On this, St. Paul writes in his second letter to the Corinthians 5:18: "All this is from God, who has reconciled us to himself through Christ, and has given us the ministry of reconciliation." In the same way, Jesus gave the Church the mandate to continue his mission of liberating the captives, healing the brokenhearted, and defending the defenseless.

---

[16] USCCB, "When I Call for Help."

Following the footsteps of Jesus, Christians are called to be ministers of reconciliation and healing.

Schreiter suggests some resources the Church can offer in the healing ministry through the reconciliation process: the healing message of the Gospel and the power of the Church's rituals.[17] Using these resources, we shall elaborate on how parish priests and Christian communities may help in the reconciliation process in the parishes. These questions will be elaborated: What message or stories of the Bible can be preached about healing that will help the abuser and the abused woman to perceive violence as a sin? What rituals can speak to the experiences of the abused and wounded women?

The Healing Message of the Gospel

The Gospel stories are words of life, hope, and love. St. Paul tells us that "while we were enemies, we were reconciled to God through the death of his Son, how much more, once reconciled, will we be saved by his life" (Romans 5:10). God proves his love for us through the death of his Son. Sins offend God and destroy our relationship with him. Thus, the reconciliation with God through his Son is a gift that ultimately comes from God. It is through Jesus that we receive reconciliation. It is also through his broken and abused body that those who suffer abuse receive healing. Schreiter explains that "the shedding of blood on the cross unto death confronts squarely the reality and the pervasiveness of violence."[18] During the time of Jesus,

---

[17] Schreiter, 1998, 127.
[18] Schreiter, 1992, 47.

death by crucifixion is an insidious form of torture and a shameful experience. Jesus went through this shameful experience to atone for our sins and reconcile us with God.

However, the cross is no longer a symbol of death and shame but rather a symbol of life and victory for those who believe in Christ. Because death on the cross brought life, it follows that before reconciliation takes place, there has to be some form of death that would lead to life. This death could be the demise of the false story that beclouds the true identity and selfhood of the victim of abuse. The false story has to die so that a redemptive narrative may emerge. Jesus reconciled us to God not only by his death and resurrection, but also by his liberating actions and messages. Before he began his public ministry, Jesus declared his mission statement: "The Spirit of the Lord is upon me, because he has anointed me to bring good news to the poor. He has sent me to proclaim release to the captives and recovery of sight to the blind, to let the oppressed go free, and to proclaim the year of the Lord's favor" (Luke 4:18-19). To achieve this mission statement, Jesus went about doing good (Acts 10:38), especially to the despised in the society. In fact, women, whose status in Israel was of inferior position, were the beneficiaries of Jesus' liberating mission.

Schreiter explains that "a spirituality of reconciliation carefully collects the shard of a shattered existence, and helps the victims piece them together as best as they can."[19] The gospel passages reveal many victims of discrimination whose stories were shattered and reshaped through social and religious discrimination. Their encounter with

---

[19] Schreiter, 1998, 38.

Jesus transformed their lives, and they were graced with new lives, new narratives, reconciliation, and healing. Three stories from the gospel will be used to expatiate how Jesus, a victim of torture, reconciles people to God and helps them find redeeming stories rather than the narrative of the lies that were imposed on them by society. The stories include, the healing of the Canaanite woman's daughter (Matthew 15:21-28), the healing of the crippled woman (Luke 13:10-17), and the encounter of Jesus with the Samaritan woman (John 4:1-42).

The Healing of the Canaanite Woman's Daughter in Matthew 15:21-28

> *Jesus left that place and went away to the district of Tyre and Sidon. Just then a Canaanite woman from that region came out and started shouting, 'Have mercy on me, Lord, Son of David; my daughter is tormented by a demon.' But he did not answer her at all. And his disciples came and urged him, saying, 'Send her away, for she keeps shouting after us.' He answered, 'I was sent only to the lost sheep of the house of Israel.' But she came and knelt before him, saying, 'Lord, help me.' He answered, 'It is not fair to take the children's food and throw it to the dogs.' She said, 'Yes, Lord, yet even the dogs eat the crumbs that fall from their masters' table.' Then Jesus answered her, 'Woman, great is your faith! Let it be done for you as you wish.' And her daughter was healed instantly.* (NRSV)

The healing occurred at Tyre and Sidon, a Gentile town. Matthew, redacting the Marcan version of the story, writes that the woman was a Canaanite. Because the nameless woman was from a despised tribe, she was looked down upon, evidenced by the disciples and Jesus' attitude toward her. The Canaanite woman was disadvantaged in several ways. For example, a woman (an inferior being), a Gentile (not allowed to relate with the Jews), and her daughter was possessed by an evil spirit (which rendered her unclean). The shame of all these traits could have changed her true story to an alternative story of a lie. Her true identity as God's beloved daughter, a human with dignity and respect, was changed to a nameless and unclean Canaanite woman by her association with her daughter. Because an evil spirit possessed her daughter, the woman could have suffered isolation and rejection by her household. Nevertheless, she had an outstanding faith and knew that Jesus was the vehicle of finding a redemptive narrative and healing.

The woman's "coming out" to meet Jesus is symbolic. It is the first step in the reconciliation process and breaking down the barrier that changed her true story. The woman addresses Jesus as "Lord" and "Son of David" – titles that even the disciples of little faith were not able to profess. Although here a non-Jew addresses Jesus as Lord and Son of David, it is shocking to watch Jesus snub the Canaanite woman in spite of her proclamation of faith. Perhaps, Jesus is trying to see whether this proclamation is from her heart. The disciples see her as a nuisance and an outsider from a wrong race and gender. They urged Jesus to send her away. Consequently, the woman's struggle to seek the help of Jesus causes her to persevere for her daughter's healing. She will not take no or rejection for an answer. To demonstrate that she actually knows who Jesus is, she kneels before Jesus and cries even more. Her kneeling is another gesture of humility, of social inferiority, and that of a client seeking a favor from a patron.[20]

Jesus' response to this humble gesture, "It is not fair to take the children's food and throw it to the dogs" (Mt. 15:26), is not only negative but also very offensive. Michael Fallon suggests that the remark might be a traditional anti-Gentile proverb common among Jews and one that the woman would understand.[21] The language of Jesus here is insulting and abusive. Amazingly, the woman does not walk away. Rather, with faith, she welcomes the humiliation of Jesus and reminds him that even the dogs eat the crumbs that fall from their master's table. Her argument is solid, forceful, and valid even as she affirms Jesus' insult. Although she intends only to eat the crumbs, she ends up with real food and dines at the table with Jesus. She is no longer an outsider, a Gentile, or an oppressed woman, but a member of the "fictive kinship" that Jesus heads.[22] Her false story is replaced with a redeemed and new story: she has become a member of Jesus's oikos (household). Faith in Jesus facilitates the Canaanite woman's

---

[20] Kerry Dearborn, "Matthew" in *The IVP Women's Bible Commentary*, ed. Catherine Kroeger and Mary Evans (Downers Grove, IL: Inter Varsity Press, 2002), 534.

[21] Michael Fallon, *The Gospel According to Matthew: An Introductory Commentary* (Bangalore, India: Asian Trading Corporation, 2002), 223.

[22] Mary Margaret Pazdan, *Becoming God's Beloved in the Company of Friends: A Spirituality of the Fourth Gospel* (Eugene, OR: Cascade Books, 2007), 62.

membership in this fictive kinship as she reclaims her place at the table.

Just as the Canaanite woman came to meet Jesus in faith and with much courage, so are all women living in abusive relationships called to do because an elephant is not overly burdened by its trunk, says an African proverb. The Canaanite woman persevered and persisted in asking that the abused women should also find a way to redeem their distorted stories. The Canaanite woman was willing to beg in public, to do homage, and to be humiliated to save her daughter and to redeem her story. Victims of abuse should not dwell in self-pity and remain in abusive relationships. They should no longer eat the crumbs under or from the table; rather, they must join the festive meal at the table, of which Jesus is the host. It is time to rise and bring to the awareness of abusive husbands that the dignity of women is to be respected. Although the problem of abuse may not be solved quickly, victims of abuse must persevere and fight for their rights so as to reclaim their places at the table.

Jesus and the Crippled Woman in Luke 13:10-17

Now, he was teaching in one of the synagogues on the Sabbath. And just then, there appeared a woman with a spirit that had crippled her for eighteen years. She was bent over and was quite unable to stand up straight. When Jesus saw her, he called her over and said, 'Woman, you are set free from your ailment.' When he laid his hands on her, immediately she stood up straight and began praising God. But the leader of the synagogue, indignant because Jesus had cured on the Sabbath, kept saying to the crowd, 'There are six days on which work ought to be done; come on those days and be cured, and not on the Sabbath day.' But the Lord answered him and said, 'You hypocrites! Does not each of you on the Sabbath untie his ox or his donkey from the manger, and lead it away to give it water? And ought not this woman, a daughter of Abraham whom Satan bound for eighteen long years, be set free from this bondage on the Sabbath day?' When he said this, all his opponents were put to shame; and the entire crowd was rejoicing at all the wonderful things that he was doing. (NRSV)

Luke's Gospel has always been described as the good news for the outcast, the poor, the sinners, the powerless, the widows, and the oppressed, and these are mostly women. It may also be the favorite Gospel for those whose stories are rewritten with falsehood. It is not as if other gospels are not for the poor, but Luke recognizes that Jesus is a universal and liberating Savior, both for the Jews and the Gentiles. Luke presents Jesus as a radical prophet who will go to any length to usher in the Reign of God. The healing story of the crippled woman is one of those acts of compassion which shows that the mission of Jesus is to raise the lowly and restore their dignity.

The setting of this healing story is the synagogue on a Sabbath day while Jesus was teaching as was his custom (Luke 4:16). The pericope presents the woman as "just appearing." It is unclear whether she was among the audience listening to Jesus. However, every pious Jew is expected to be in the synagogue on the Sabbath. Probably, like every other Jew, this woman had simply come to worship without expecting any healing. Although she could not properly see Jesus since she was bent over and could not stand upright, she was at a strategic place where Jesus noticed that her affliction was not natural. She had suffered rejection and false story for eighteen years. Her true story of the dignified daughter of Abraham must have changed to a false narrative because she could neither stand upright nor join others in proper worship and because her ill health was attributed to an evil spirit. Thus, she was automatically rendered unclean and could have faced rejection and ridicule for eighteen years.

Evidently, in Israel, sicknesses were attributed either to sin or to the attack of the evil spirit (Luke 4:33; 6:18; 7:21; 8:2). No wonder Jesus initiated the healing when he saw her condition: "Woman, you are set free from your ailment." Jesus touched her and healed her. Her regular coming to the synagogue was a sign that she sought God and that she believed that her burden would be over someday, although it took eighteen years. She came to the synagogue to praise God, and she never ceased to glorify God when she recognized that the power within Jesus to restore her health and her identity was actually from God.

The synagogue leader expressed a negative reaction to this healing. Clearly revealing his indignant reaction to the crowd, the synagogue leader focused on the issue of the violation of the Sabbath law by quoting from Exodus 20:9-10: "There are six days when work should be done; come on those days and be cured, and not on the Sabbath day." With his argument, the synagogue leader thought that he was making a legal point, which, of course, he was. However, Jesus did not spare him from his sarcastic remarks, and he ought to have realized that a tree that encourages a bird to nest on it should be prepared for its leaves to be shattered. Jesus has the right answers for his satirical and pharisaic argument. In response, Jesus calls him a hypocrite and makes an argument from the lesser to the greater, (*argumentum ad maius*), i.e., comparing the ox and donkey with the woman. That is to say, if a donkey or an ox bound for a few hours can be loosed on a Sabbath, how much more is this daughter of Abraham, who was bound for eighteen years? Barbara Reid, a feminist scripture scholar, explains that since the Sabbath was created for the praise of God and the liberation of humanity, the healing of the bent-over woman fulfills the Sabbath because she was enabled to praise God more fully.[23] Accordingly, this healing on a Sabbath is not a disobedience to the law of the Sabbath as is interpreted by the synagogue leader, but rather the true application of the law.

Ultimately, Jesus' address to this woman as "a daughter of Abraham" is very significant. This honor places the woman back in the covenantal community and within the Reign of God. Her honor and dignity are restored because the claim of Abraham as an ancestor is the pride of every Jew. The honor bestowed on the healed woman is certainly a reversal of her former status. She has a new story of redemption, different from the false story that defames her true identity. She can stand upright and worship God with her fellow Jews. Her purity, dignity, and respect are restored since she is free from the bondage of Satan and can be proudly called the daughter of Abraham.

---

[23] Barbara Reid, "Sabbath, the Crown of Creation," in *Earth, Wind, and Fire: Biblical and Theological Perspectives on Creation*, ed. Carol Dempsey and Mary Margaret Pazdan (Collegeville, MN: Liturgical Press, 2004), 73.

Jesus' Encounter with the Samaritan Woman in John 4:1-42

Jesus left Judea and started back to Galilee. But he had to go through Samaria. So he came to a Samaritan city called Sychar, near the plot of ground that Jacob had given to his son Joseph. Jacob's well was there, and Jesus, tired out by his journey, was sitting by the well. It was about noon. A Samaritan woman came to draw water, and Jesus said to her, 'Give me a drink'. (His disciples had gone to the city to buy food.) The Samaritan woman said to him, 'How is it that you, a Jew, ask a drink of me, a woman of Samaria?' (Jews do not share things in common with Samaritans.) Jesus answered her, 'If you knew the gift of God, and who it is that is saying to you, "Give me a drink", you would have asked him, and he would have given you living water.' The woman said to him, 'Sir, you have no bucket, and the well is deep. Where do you get that living water? Are you greater than our ancestor Jacob, who gave us the well, and with his sons and his flocks drank from it?' Jesus said to her, Everyone who drinks of this water will be thirsty again, but those who drink of the water that I will give them will never be thirsty. The water that I will give will become in them a spring of water gushing up to eternal life.' The woman said to him, 'Sir, give me this water, so that I may never be thirsty or have to keep coming here to draw water.' Jesus said to her, 'Go, call your husband, and come back.' The woman answered him, 'I have no husband.' Jesus said to her, 'You are right in saying, "I have no husband"; for you have had five husbands, and the one you have now is not your husband. What you have said is true!' The woman said to him, 'Sir, I see that you are a prophet. Our ancestors worshipped on this mountain, but you say that the place where people must worship is in Jerusalem.' Jesus said to her, 'Woman, believe me, the hour is coming when you will worship the Father neither on this mountain nor in Jerusalem. You worship what you do not know; we worship what we know, for salvation is from the Jews. But the hour is coming, and is now here, when the true worshippers will worship the Father in spirit and truth, for the Father seeks such as these to worship him. God is spirit, and those who worship him must worship in spirit and truth.' The woman said to him, 'I know that Messiah is coming' (who is called Christ). 'When he comes, he will proclaim all things to us.' Jesus said to her, 'I am he, the one who is speaking to you.' Just then, his disciples came. They were astonished that he was speaking with a woman, but no one said, 'What do you want?' or, 'Why are you speaking with her?' Then, the woman left her water jar and went back to the city. She said to the people, 'Come and see a man who told me everything I have ever done! He cannot be the Messiah, can he?' They left the city and were on their way to him.... Many Samaritans from that city believed in him because of the woman's testimony, 'He told me everything I have ever done.' (NRSV)

At the well of Jacob in a Samaritan city – Sychar, Jesus, and his disciples were on their way to Galilee, but they had to pass through a Gentile town. The Samaritan woman had come to draw water, and

Jesus engaged in a conversation with her. As a foreigner, it was a scandal for Jesus to speak with her and, worse still, to ask her for water.[24] But Jesus was tired and thirsty. Hence, his condition prompted a conversation with a woman with whom he was not supposed to talk under the law. False narratives also surrounded this woman, and her stories of the lie could go this way: she is an outsider, a despicable person in her community, her character is questionable, she is alone at the well at an odd hour, she had married five husbands when the Law of Moses frowned on more than three marriages.[25] She engaged in a conversation with a strange man in a public place. These narratives of the lie replaced her true story as a child of God worthy of respect. She needed a new story, and her encounter with Jesus provided an opportunity for her transformation.

Both Jesus and the Samaritan woman had a need: Jesus thirsted for her faith, and the woman thirsted for what she did not know. However, she is aware that the mercy of God is welling up in her, which is the beginning of her reconciliation process. The woman also is courageous enough to engage in a theological conversation with Jesus. Moved with faith, she asks Jesus a pressing theological question that divided the Jews and the Samarians: Where is the proper place to worship God?[26] Jesus not only revealed the manner of wor-

---

[24] Francis Moloney, *The Gospel of John, Sacra Pagina Series* vol. 4, ed. Daniel Harrington (Collegeville, MN: The Liturgical Press, 1998), 116.

[25] Dianne Bergant, and Richard Fragomeni, *Preaching the New Lectionary: Year A* (Collegeville, MN: The Liturgical Press, 2001), 101.

[26] Gail O'Day, "John," in *Women's Bible Commentary*, ed. Carol Newsom and Sharon Ringe (Louisville, KY: Westminster John Knox Press, 1998), 384.

Chapter 4: Genuine Healing through the Process of Reconciliation

ship pleasing to God, but also revealed his identity as the expected Christ. After experiencing Jesus, the woman's spiritual thirst was quenched and refreshed. Her story of the lie gave way to a new and redemptive narrative. She left her jar and became a witness of the good news to her people.

Why did she leave behind her jar, and what is the significance of this action? What happened at that well? The jar could be her old lifestyle. Her ability to confront her situation through the grace of God brought a new and redemptive story. Certainly, a loving heart spoke to a broken heart to mend, heal, and give it life. Because the Samaritan woman was open to the transformation Jesus was offering, the barrier between the insider and the outsider was broken, her loneliness was healed, and her true self and dignity were restored. She became a voice that witnessed Jesus to his people who would never have listened to her under normal circumstances.

The commonality of these Stories and their Application

These three stories have many things in common. In each story, Jesus is the reconciler of the victim to himself and the community. All these women had stories of lies that branded them as outcasts and lowered their self-esteem, dignity, and respect. These false stories had to die so that a true and redemptive story could emerge. However, the reconciliation process began with each of them and the grace of God working in and through them. The Canaanite woman had strong faith, courage, and humility to meet Jesus in public without minding the consequences. The crippled woman had faith in God and had frequented the synagogue for eighteen years, waiting for God to act. The Samaritan woman believed in her ancestors' God and was hoping for the Messiah who would deliver her from her lowly position. Their encounters with Jesus brought transformation, reconciliation, healing, and the beginning of their redemptive stories. Their experiences imply that reconciliation is a spiritual journey, brought about by God through Jesus. Nevertheless, the victim of violence has to cooperate with the grace of God working within her.

Pastoral ministers can use the stories of these great women in their reconciliation process and in giving the victims of abuse hope and an optimistic spirit. The message of Jesus is the good news of liberation, joy, hope, love, deliverance, acceptance, and respect for human dignity. Preaching with them will create an environment that will move the victims of violence to seek reconciliation with Jesus, with themselves, and with the abuser.

Jesus still reconciles all people to himself through his Body, the Church. The Church is aware that many of its female members are wounded through abuse even though they are hiding their plights in good dresses and hats. These women are passive and helpless in their situations. They need to hear through the Church that they can regain their wounded humanity again. In other words, these victims have to become conscious of the effects of violence, represented in the narrative of the lie, in their lives. Consequently, they must seek the mercy of God and lament for help to be healed. The Church is the instrument through which a wounded woman can come to realize the damage done to her story. It is through the liturgy that most wounded women encounter Jesus. However, both the abuser and the abused need to hear the Word of God preached to them. They need to hear the call to freedom, liberation, and healing through the voice of the Church.

James Newton Poling, a theologian and professor of pastoral care and counseling, concurs that perpetrators of family violence need to hear that God hates violence.[27] Similarly, during the World Meeting of Families in September 2015 at Philadelphia, USA, a psychologist, Christauria Welland, gave a talk captioned "When the Wound Comes From Within: Domestic Violence in Catholic Families;" she encouraged the church leaders to speak out against domestic violence. Welland explained: "The church leaders and ministers also could speak out more against domestic violence, even at the pulpit. I often think that the moral authority of priests and bishops goes to waste in this area because there's so much they could say that would make such a huge difference. When they do that, it's a huge opportunity to help families, just by making that statement so everybody is clear on what is and is not right."[28] In every parish, the pastors use the pulpit to reveal the revelation in the Word of God. How will a shift in pulpit preaching help to illuminate both the good news of the scriptures and shed healing light for victims of abuse? In order words, how might the pastors preach the stories of the Canaanite or the Samaritan woman (or any related scriptural passage) and con-

---

[27] James N. Poling, "Preaching to Perpetrators of Violence," in *Telling the Truth: Preaching about Sexual and Domestic Violence*, ed. John McClure and Nancy Ramsay (Cleveland, OH: United Church Press, 1998), 71.

[28] Laura Ieraci, "Expert: Healing possible for victims, perpetrators of domestic violence" *The Catholic Register*, Posted September 28, 2015, www.catholicregister.org/faith/faith-news/item/20985-expert-healing-for-victims-perpetrators-of-domestic-violence.

nect them with the experiences of the abused women so that these stories impart upon the wounded listeners the need to seek reconciliation? What if the said liturgy's opening prayer (collect) and the prayer of the faithful also reflect the healing needed by the victims of abuse in society?

Similarly, the Psalms can also become uplifting laments for abused women, especially Psalm 31. "Be gracious to me, O LORD, for I am in distress; with grief, my eyes are wasted, my soul and body spent. For my life is worn out by sorrow, and my years by sighing. My strength fails in affliction, and my bones are consumed" (Ps. 31:10-11). When Psalms of lament are preached in the context of the experiences of domestic abuse, an injured woman can relate to it as she cries or laments to God.

Unfortunately, most battered women also use the scripture to justify their inferiority and subordination to their husband's abuse.[29] An oppressed woman is likely to validate the abuse with much conviction: "It might be God's will that I suffer, 'for God chastises those he loves'" (Hebrew 12:6). "It is my duty to serve my husband and keep my family together, 'for what God has joined together, only death can put asunder'" (Mark 10:9). "This might be my own cross for Jesus says, 'Take up your cross and follow me'" (Matthew 16:24). Although suffering and crosses may visit an individual without invitation, it is necessary to question some injustices that are inflicted on victims of abuse. This saying reminded me of an anecdote from African culture: "Once upon a time, Suffering came knocking on the door of an unfortunate victim. This individual says, "Please do not

---

[29] Clarke, 69.

come in, for I have no seat for you. Suffering replied: "Don't worry, I brought my seat." That is to say when an uninvited misery visits a person, it comes with chains of problems. For this reason, the Psalmist begged God: "Please, God, balance with joy the years when we knew misfortune" (Ps. 90:15). Everyone deserves to be happy, even in the midst of our broken society. A married woman deserves to enjoy her married life rather than languish in sorrow with chains of abuse. No wonder an African proverb tells us that it is better to be happy in a poor shack or hut than to be sad in the palace of a bully king. I concur that being happy in a poor, peaceful family is superior and healthier than being a queen in a family of cruelty.

Nonetheless, exposing the evils of patriarchal culture, of male superiority, and naming domestic abuse as a sin within the liturgy can prompt these women to question their belief and justification of the abuse. The victims of abuse might likely gain the courage to speak out to begin the process of reconciliation. Accordingly, the abusers cannot rationalize their sinful behavior when it is authoritatively condemned from the pulpit and when the scripture is used to hold them accountable for their sins, especially from the prophet Ezekiel: "The soul that sins shall die" (Ez. 18:19-21). They may no longer see a woman as a property or a thing to be used. And the abused themselves may begin to see the need for a redemptive story.

Apart from using scriptural messages to condemn oppressive behavior, the Church also has rich documents and official teachings on the equality of the human person, women's dignity, and family life, as mentioned in chapter two. These documents of the Church need to be used properly in the parishes because violence against women has become a pastoral issue in the Church. Clergymen need to be vigilant and guard the sheep in their care, even when they are silent, because telling their stories may be embarrassing. Battered women and their oppressors need to hear about the documents of the Church that condemn discrimination and abuse, especially from the pulpit.

Obviously, telling the truth about the effects of violence from the pulpit can move even those women who are suffering in silence to speak up and seek for assistance. Married couples who are having crises in their union need to hear frequently about the equality of men and women, mutual love, and interdependent relationships. There is need also to emphasize the respect and love that Jesus had for women as demonstrated in many gospel stories: the woman caught in adultery (John 8:1-11), the woman who washed the feet of Jesus (Luke 7:36-50), the widow of Nain (Luke 7:11-17), the story of the widow's mite (Mark 12:41-44), the women who supported the ministry of Jesus (Luke 8:1-3), etc. Jesus is our role model for the reconciliation ministry because he seeks the respect and dignity of every person, both women and men.

The spirituality of reconciliation in which Jesus empowers the Church to engage is not built on the exercise of dominative power; rather, it is a reconciliation that sees the trauma of the abused and takes her to a new place and a new story. Schreiter notes that the quest for the spirituality of reconciliation that calls for non-violent alternatives creates space for surprises to happen. The Church is missioned to create this space that can help abused women to piece together their shattered existence carefully. As effective ministers of reconciliation and healing, the clergy must continue with the mission of liberation of Jesus, which is the ability to create new spaces that are safe for the victims of abuse to revisit their memories of trauma and reweave them into a new story.[30] The church can equally use prayerful support and rituals in the healing process. Below are some rituals and their powerful effects.

The Power of Ritual in the Healing Process

Ritual expresses deeply what our language cannot articulate. Schreiter explains that ritual is a "moment of transition in the reconciliation process which gives expression to feelings so painful and so deep that no other way can be found to bear the feelings."[31] Intimidation, threats, and abuse are often so horrible that they cannot be verbally expressed. Rituals can help victims get in touch with these feelings. Schreiter admits that we cannot understand entirely how ritual works, but it is often a moment of grace for the abused woman. He continues that the "repetitive, ritualistic process untangles the skein of a false story and opens up new perspectives."[32] When the support group gathers for their bi-weekly or monthly meetings, the session can be concluded with a prayerful ritual. Ritualizing their experiences is another avenue through which they can mourn their wounds and pains in a deeper and non-verbal way. Each group member can take turns preparing and leading the group during this ritual or prayer service. Leading the group can inspire and empower each

---

[30] Schreiter, 1992, 36-38.
[31] Ibid., 75.
[32] Schreiter, 1998, 93.

woman to be creative, and she can be graced to relate the prayerful ritual to her personal experiences.

A concrete example of the importance of prayer service among the victims of abuse can be illustrated with my ministry experience at the Home for Abused Women and Children in the USA. During this time, I realized that rituals helped many victims of abuse. These women gathered in a circle every Wednesday to ritualize their experiences, during which deep feelings that were not disclosed under normal circumstances would be expressed. One of the rituals we performed together with the women was entitled "Healing Through Grieving our Losses." We gathered around a ritual space with lit candles and turned off the electric lights. The space was very quiet. I encouraged the women to be present to themselves, enter our worship space, and reflect on the word grief. I gave them a short reflection on the story of the widow of Nain, whose only son died in Luke 7:11-17. We paused to reflect on the gospel story. After a few minutes of silence, I asked them to express spontaneously in a few phrases what grief meant to them, the losses in their lives, how they had grieved or not in the past, and what they needed to mourn or let go of. After our sharing, I brought a bowl of water. I asked those who were willing to wash their hands in the bowl and to do so as a symbol of relinquishing the burden of losses in their lives. This washing was done prayerfully and slowly as I reminded them of their baptismal experiences and how we became beloved daughters of God through the waters of baptism (especially for those who were Christians). During the prayerful washing of their hands, these wounded women cried so bitterly that evening, and later, they confessed how the ritual brought healing to them and how the process relieved much of the burden they were carrying.

Apart from the support group rituals or prayer service, the Church has rich sacramental rituals such as the Eucharist and the Sacrament of Reconciliation. The Eucharist is the greatest ritual for Catholics since it is the source and summit of our faith. Schreiter explains that at the Eucharistic table, "the broken and the abused bodies of individual victims and the broken body of the Church are taken up into the body of Christ which knew torture and shame."[33] The Eucharist is the real and enduring presence of Christ: "And remember, I am with you always to the end of the age" (Mt. 28:20). Moreover, in the Eucharistic celebration, we recall the memory of the passion and death of Jesus who suffered and died on the cross. Christ's self-emptying and sacrificial love and his utter trust in the will of God made him embrace the cross. In the wounds of Christ, the victims of abuse rediscover their true story, their identity, and their humanity. The redeeming story every priest can offer to the wounded women during Mass is for them to find solace in the broken body of Christ symbolized in the bread that is broken at the altar.

The Sacrament of Reconciliation is another ritual of the Church that can bring healing to the victims of abuse and the abuser as well. But before the traditional private confession, the parish priest can plan a public reconciliation service with guided meditation. The scriptural passage that speaks about grief, hope, forgiveness, healing, love, faith, freedom, justice, or reconciliation can be read for reflection during this meditation. The abuser and his victim present will

---

[33] Schreiter, 1992, 75.

be listening and praying with any of the scriptural passages chosen by the priest as he or any lay leader guides the assembly on the message of the Bible. The passage can also be connected with the experiences of abuse in order to show how unjust and sinful violence is. Some passages can also emphasize the joy of living in peace and love. This guided reflection may help the abused to confront her stories of injustice, the intimidations she faced, and the painful effects of abuse, thus creating space for healing, justice, and new possibilities. The aim of the meditation is to move the abused to lament over her false story, to seek reconciliation and relationship with self and with God, and to cultivate trust, good self-esteem, and a redemptive story. At the end of this meditation, the pastor can hear the private confessions of those who requested absolution.

The rituals, the scriptural messages, and the compassionate listening heart of the Church can be sources of empowerment for the victims of abuse. The abuser can also be transformed from abusive tendencies through the reconciliation rituals and through the gospel message that condemns and holds him accountable for his sins. Jesus, however, did not come to condemn us but to give us abundant life (Jn. 10:10). Thus, both the abuser and the abused need this eternal life. In Evangelii nuntiandi, Pope Paul VI wrote that the Church is made up of imperfect members who are in need of constant conversion and evangelization (no. 15). Therefore, men who indulge in the sin of abuse, even as they are held responsible for their actions, must also be brought to the healing banquet of Christ.

This chapter has explained how the Church can become an effective minister of healing through the reconciliation process and through the breaking of the Word of God that will awaken in the abuse the need to seek the true story of her life. It also explained what healing is, what forgiveness does in the healing process, the importance of ritualizing wounded experiences, and how the sacraments of confession and the Eucharist can bring healing to the victims of abuse as well as the repentance of the abuser. The next chapter will suggest the way forward in abating the regular occurrences of domestic violence.

Chapter 5

Recommendations

"Until exclusion and inequality in society and between peoples are reversed, it will be impossible to eliminate violence."

—Pope Francis, *The Joy of the Gospel*

Healing, forgiveness, and reconciliation are spiritual gifts from God that victims of abuse desire to experience. The previous chapter has proposed some of the resources and actions the Church can take to bring about healing – preaching the healing message of the Gospels, the power of rituals, and the formation of support groups. This chapter will suggest recommendations that will aid in minimizing the regular occurrences of domestic violence in families. These recommendations are both pastoral and civil, and they include: the formulation of prayer against violence, the need for a pastoral letter from the Catholic African Bishops to condemn domestic abuse as a sin, the need for the clergy to preach the gospel using the lens of Jesus, the empowerment of women through solidarity groups, and the need for civil authority to make domestic violence illegal in all African countries.

Formulation of Prayer against Domestic Violence

Towards the end of the twentieth century, the Nigerian Catholic bishops composed two prayers in 1993—Prayer for Nigeria in Distress and Prayer Against Bribery and Corruption in Nigeria. These national prayers were evidence that Nigerian bishops had the interest of the Nigerian society at heart, which is the same in all African countries. In the same way, the African bishops could come up with a prayer against domestic violence either as an individual nation or as an African Church. The prayer against domestic violence can be prayed during Sunday Masses in every parish after the reception of Holy Communion. The goal of the prayer is to ask for healing for the victims of abuse and to bring to the awareness of the abuser the enormous horror of domestic violence experience. The prayer may help the victims of abuse know that they are not alone in their suffering and implant in them the desire to seek reconciliation and healing. Through this prayer, the abuser may understand that domestic violence is sinful and that he needs to repent from oppressive behavior.

Below is an example of the proposed prayer against domestic abuse:

> Gracious and loving God, your plan for humanity is to be in relationships of mutual love, interdependence, equality, and respect. We, your people, are sorry for not cherishing your gift of love, and in many ways, we have abused others physically, emotionally, sexually, culturally, economically, or spiritually. We repent of our wickedness and sin, acknowledging that domestic violence is evil. Lord, listen to our prayer and

grant healing to men, women, and children who live with the trauma of abuse. Keep them safe from the threat of hatred and restore their dignity and peace of mind. Grant the victims of abuse the grace to seek liberation and reconciliation that comes from You alone. Lord be their strength, refuge, and companion. Help the perpetrators of violence to understand the impact of hostility on the victims of abuse. Awaken in the abusers the desire to seek equity, justice, and fairness in their relationships and realize that violent behavior opposes and destroys your plan for humanity. We make our prayer through Christ our Lord. Amen.

Pastoral Letter from the Bishops

It is evident from this paper that the most common form of violence against women occurs at the family level, and the Church is cognizant of this reality. As explained above, John Paul II noted that "[w]omen's dignity has often been unacknowledged and their prerogatives misrepresented" ("Letter to Women," no. 3). The Nigerian bishops also recognized in 2002 the commercialization of sex among young Nigerian women who were taken to Europe for a disguised job. Following this revelation, the Nigerian bishops wrote a pastoral letter to condemn this atrocity. The pastoral letter entitled "Restoring the Dignity of the Nigerian Woman" came about because the bishops saw a problem, and they addressed it.[1]

---

[1] Catholic Bishop's Conference Nigeria, 2002, 2.

Similarly, the Church in Africa needs a pastoral letter from the bishops to condemn and respond to domestic violence that is destroying many homes. The Church is aware that women's dignity is often not acknowledged and that some women suffer much abuse at home; however, little is done to combat this sin. The family is the domestic church. Anything that affects its foundation will automatically affect the Mother Church. Thus, writing a pastoral letter to condemn violence at home will not destroy the institution of marriage; on the other hand, this letter will strengthen the marriage bond and improve interpersonal relationships, love, and respect. Following the example of the United States Catholic bishops' pastoral response to domestic violence, "When I Call for Help,"[2] the African bishops could write a pastoral letter to condemn the evils of domestic abuse. St. John Paul II explains that "to be human is to be called to interpersonal communion, and marriage is the fundamental dimension of this call."[3] Abuse of one's spouse negates this call and thus should be preached as an aspect of sin. The response to domestic abuse, through the proposed pastoral letter, is based on the act of love for humanity and the belief in the dignity of the human person in whom we see the face of Christ.

---

[2] United States Conference of Catholic Bishops, "When I Call for Help: A Pastoral Response to Domestic Violence Against Women," November 12, 2002.

[3] John Paul II, *Mulieris dignitatem*, no. 7, Libreria Editrice Vaticana, August 15, 1998, www. vatican.va/holy_father/john_paul_ii/apost_letters/documents/hf_jp-ii_apl_15081988_mulieria-dignitatem_en.html, no. 7.

Interpretation of the Scripture using the Lens of Jesus

In their pastoral response to domestic violence, the U. S. bishops write: "As bishops, we condemn the use of the Bible to support abusive character in any form. A correct reading of scripture leads people to an understanding of the equal dignity of men and women and relationships based on mutuality and love."[4] The use of scriptural passages, especially the creation of Eve from the ribs of Adam or St. Paul's admonitions to relegate women to the background, does not give life. Women and men are created for mutual love, respect, interpersonal relationships, and mutual complementarities. The Catechism of the Catholic Church explains: "Man and woman have been created, which is to say, willed by God: on the one hand, in perfect equality as human persons; on the other, in their respective beings as man and woman" (CCC, no. 369). Clearly, from this Catholic social teaching, it is apparent that the Church's admonition endorses the dignity and equality of all persons because they possess and share the same nature and humanity created in God's image. Both males and females are created by God, for God, as well as for each other. The ability of people to live together in service to one another and for the common good stems from the dignity, unity, and equality of all people.

In interpreting the scripture, the lens of Jesus can be applied since the message of Jesus is that of hope, liberation, love, and reconciliation. He condemned the atrocities of the people of his time without fear or favor. His actions defended the dignity of women.

---

[4] USCCB, "When I Call for Help."

Many instances abound in the scripture: During Jesus' encounter with the Samaritan woman, the disciples were surprised that Jesus was talking with a woman (John 4:27). The Pharisee who invited Jesus for dinner marveled that a sinner was touching Jesus and yet Jesus did not condemn her (Luke 7:39). The woman caught in adultery, who was to be stoned to death, was delivered by Jesus (John 8:3-11). The unclean woman who had suffered hemorrhage for twelve years rendered Jesus unclean by touching him; Jesus did not condemn her, but he declared her faith great (Mark 5:25-34).

In the same way, the members of the clergy are to use Jesus' model in interpreting the scripture and properly explaining that scriptural messages should not be used to justify discrimination. Interestingly, some perpetrators of violence quote the scriptural passages to insist that their victims forgive them, e. G., "Jesus commands us to forgive seventy-seven times" (Mt. 18:22). When the scripture is quoted, the victim feels guilty because of her inability to forgive. The wound is deep and hurts so much that the victim is even helpless and passive. Treating forgiveness as an action that has to be carried out by the victim of abuse does not work. This was discussed earlier on reconciliation as a hasty peace. As stated above, forgiveness is a gift from God that takes time. Forgiveness is recognizing that the injured woman is human. However, before the victim is graced to forgive, the victim and the abuser must be aware of the brutal consequences of abuse. The abuser must be accountable for his actions, and the abused must go through the process of reconciliation.

Often, the victims of abuse perceive the abuse as their cross or as the will of God for them and use the Bible to justify this claim, as explained previously. The abusers themselves claim that violent behavior is a loss of control or a temptation by the evil one, rather than a choice and a deliberate use of power and control. Indeed, the will of God for everyone is to be happy and to experience God's love through one another. Inasmuch as every loving relationship might face challenges from time to time, when abuse becomes a regular incident that threatens the life of a partner, then the couples need help. Certainly, marriage is permanent; nevertheless, when there is no relationship of love, peace, or joy in a union, the couples can either seek help to restore their marital love or mourn the loss of the relationship through an annulment process.

Formation of Solidarity Groups for Women in the Society

The popular saying has it that solidarity is power. For generations, solidarity groups have liberated women from the power imbalance between men and women. A Kikuyu (one of the tribes in Kenya) proverb states that when one walks alone, no one will bother to pave the way for him/her. But if it is a group walk, everyone paves the way for them. Working as a group, though it has its own shortcomings, may be very helpful to the plight of the wounded victims of abuse because it helps women to share their experiences from which they get support/comfort and become stronger as they find solace and consolation from others' stories. On the importance of group solidarity, I will refer to a story by Bishop Shanahan, the Holy Ghost clergyman who brought Catholicism to south-eastern Nigeria. The bishop explained:

In a certain village in Igbo land, the men raised pigs as the traditional sacrifice to the god (Odo). The women of this village grew cassava and cocoyam, and the pigs liked to feast on them. However, these crops were the source of income for the women. The women tolerated this injustice for a while and decided to embark on a mass protest, which did not work out. Under the influence of their leader, the women of this community held a meeting and came up with another plan, which they kept a secret. They planned to prepare the evening meal as usual on a certain day but to starve their husbands. In a traditional Igbo society, men do not enter a woman's kitchen or serve food from the kitchen himself. Thus, on this fateful day, after preparing meals that would be enough for a week, each woman wrapped the food in a container and left her home. The men and children waited in vain to be fed, but the women were nowhere to be found. There were many days of chaos as the men battled with feeding their babies who were wailing. They were forced to enter into the kitchen to cook. The frustrated men decided to make peace with their wives and suggested that they return home voluntarily and that there would be no beating. The women vowed not to go back until the last pig in the village had been killed or sold. They asked their husbands to choose between them and the pigs. After much consultation, the men agreed to their wives' demands and sold all the pigs in their village.[5]

---

[5] Uchem, 55-57.

This story demonstrates that women usually function very well in a group, and their wishes are respected when they demonstrate on the streets of Nairobi, Lagos, Abuja, or any other city in any country. The women's group, if properly organized and structured, will become another safe place where cases of abuse are reported. (Although families living in urban areas may disapprove of this kind of group solidarity, life in the city is individualistic, and family life has changed drastically during this 21st century. But in rural areas, where communal living is predominant, women's solidarity groups are still functional). In the city, civil rights groups mostly take to the streets to advocate for one thing or another.

While some of these groups might have common interests and are formed in an ad hoc manner, others are well structured and are professional groups, for instance, FIDA-Kenya (In Spanish – Federacion Internacional de Abogadas, meaning Federation of Women Lawyers). These are high-class women in the society, and the hoi polloi, or the common masses, may not belong to this group because of class differences. The group I am advocating for, however, is where every voice counts, and all women in the community feel accepted and belong regardless of age, class, tribe, economic status, religious affiliation, etc. In this group, like the case above, when a man is reported to have molested his wife, the group will take him to court and protect the interest of the victim.

Apart from this social organization of women's groups, the leaders of these groups can persuade the government to organize public seminars to educate women on their rights to human dignity as legitimate citizens. Through solidarity groups, many women can learn about the need for education and financial empowerment. Education will empower women to know their rights; they can take appropriate actions when violated. Education will also empower them financially to care for their children even when they have to end a relationship that is not working. That some women do not reveal signs of physical abuse is probably because they have no idea about their constitutional rights and/or they are not financially capable of sustaining themselves without the man. However, when empowered, a woman can stand independently and fend for herself and her children.

The Church and the Civil Authorities

An injury a woman sustains from domestic abuse ought not to be the concern of the Church alone. The civil authority, through the police, is obliged to hold the abuser accountable for violating a human right – the right to human dignity. Unfortunately, the police sometimes regard domestic violence as a family affair rather than an infringement on a person's right, as explained above. Consequently, many women do not report the abuse to the police. They prefer to suffer in silence. The police need some training in gender issues so that matters of gender violence can be handled appropriately. The Church in Africa can work hand-in-hand with the police to see that an oppressed woman is free from the danger of being mishandled or being killed by the abuser. The Church can also foster the cause of making domestic violence illegal through civil authority.

The Nigerian constitution of 1999, for instance, guarantees "freedom from discrimination and equality of all before the law (article 17(2) and 42 (1). Despite these provisions, however, no federal laws specifically criminalize violence in the family or make violence in the family a criminal offense."[6] Articles 2, 3, 23, 24, and 26 of the Kenyan new constitution of 2010 provide protection against the discrimination of women. Article 27(3) also outlines the equal rights of men and women regarding economic, social, and cultural rights. These are all wonderful rights. However, the same Kenyan constitution on Family Protection Bill, Section 5(a) and articles 3, 7, and 10 condemn sexual abuse and domestic violence as "unacceptable behavior" but do not criminalize the abuser.[7] The implication of this is that there is no protection for the marital rape victims and the physically abused women since the abusers are not criminalized, and the police often dismiss reports of abuse as family matters.

Therefore, making domestic violence illegal and criminalizing the offender in African countries will awaken in the consciousness of men a sense of justice in family affairs and equitable gender relationships at home and in society at large. It is also necessary for civil society to provide emergency shelters that will provide accommodation, counseling, and medical care to women who are seeking shelter outside of their matrimonial homes. Some wounded women actually remain in abusive relationships when they are economically dependent on their partner and when the government facilities available

---

[6] Nikki Naylor, "Drafting Domestic Violence Legislation in Nigeria: Lessons from South Africa." Women's Legal Centre (September 2005), 9.

[7] FIDA-Kenya, "Assessment of the Implementation of the Previous Concluding Observations on Kenya (CCPR/CO/83/KEN) at the time of the Review of the Third Periodic Report," Office of the High Commissioner for Human Rights, Nairobi, Kenya, August 5, 2011, www2.ohchr.org/English/bodies/hrc/docs/ngos/FIDA_Kenya103.doc

are not sufficient. These facilities are mostly left in the hands of NGOs in many African countries. The Church can encourage the civil authority to attend to the voices of the many wounded women who are silently crying for help.

Conclusion

"Our church doors should always be open, so that if someone, moved by the Spirit, comes there looking for God, he or she will not find a closed door."

—Pope Francis, *The Joy of the Gospel*, no.47

"A frog decided to climb the top of a tree. His family members were frustrated and unhappy because they knew that it was impossible. As this frog made the first move, the rest of the frogs shouted, 'It's impossible, it's impossible!' Thinking they were encouraging him and hailing him to reach the top, the deaf frog made it to the end."

—Unknown author

From this short parable, it is obvious that the hearing impairment of the frog made it possible for it to reach its target despite the negative criticism from family members. Sometimes, it is good to become deaf to negative, unhelpful, harmful, discouraging, and pessimistic voices that destroy rather than empower people. When negative voices of: "you are no good, you cannot make it, you are not capable" are constantly communicated to the victims of abuse, many will tend to believe that they are no good indeed. My take on this is that the condition of one does not define who one is. In other words, you are not your condition. Your only disability is self-pity and a negative attitude toward life without believing in the power within you to succeed. Give a deaf ear to this self-pity so as to experience the power within you to succeed.

Augustine Igbuku, a Nigerian author, writes that life will never give you your desires in a platter of gold. You will have to rise and fight for your rights, future, family, and dreams.[1] Sometimes, we waste time chasing external validation and good recommendations that may not come our way. The courage to continue striving, love, and believe in oneself leads to transformation. But giving up on fate or negative feelings does not bring life. It is not about how many times a person falls, but how many times the said person is able to get up and continue struggling, realize that within one is the power to succeed, and say "NO" to violence and self-pity.

Unless the victim of this aggression and hostility comes to the realization that there is power within her to succeed, she might be traumatized for life.

> Once upon a time, in heaven, there was a discussion among the gods about where to hide the miraculous secret power of success by which humans can achieve anything on earth. One of the gods suggested the depth of the sea. Another was on a high mountain, and another thought of the cave in the woods. The last intelligent god said, "Keep it in the depth of the mind of human beings. They will never suspect that the power is hidden in them. This is because right from child-

---

[1] Augustine Igbuku, The Pursuit of Sterling Attitude (Oxford, UK: PubliciseJesus, 2015), 69.

hood, the mind of humanity is prone to wandering rather than looking within. Only the intelligent among them will look within, use the power, and become great."[2]

The Power within us to excel includes the right attitude towards misfortune, the willpower to arise where one has fallen rather than spend energy in self-blame and self-pity, and the determination to transform painful and violent experiences into learning experiences.

Violence is counter-productive and guarantees disharmony. In preaching for a non-violent attitude, Jesus explains: "You have heard that it was said, 'an eye for an eye and a tooth for a tooth.' But I say to you, 'do not resist an evildoer….' You have heard that it was said, 'You shall love your neighbor and hate your enemy.' But I say to you, 'Love your enemies and pray for those who persecute you, so that you may be children of your Father in heaven; for he makes his sun rise on the evil and the good, and sends rain on the righteous and the unrighteous'" (Matthew 5:38-48).

Mahatma Gandhi also used a non-violent approach to social matters. He says: "An eye for an eye only ends up making the whole world blind. Nonviolence is not a garment to be put on and off at will. Its seat is in the heart and must be an inseparable part of our being." Violence does not keep a family in peace or make for harmonious co-existence, nor does it accord honor and dignity to a cruel head of the family. Amazingly, anyone who is destined for power does not struggle for it. That is, respect, honor, reverence, high esteem, and admiration do not come with brutality and cruelty. Vio-

---

[2] Gupte, 10.

lence rather belittles the status of the one who uses it as an avenue to make his presence felt in the family or community.

Violence begets violence! says Martin Luther King Jr. He suggested that the forces of hatred must be met with the forces of love. Apparently, this attitude is not as easy as it sounds. It takes courage. It takes grace from God. It takes prayer. It takes willpower and a genuine decision to say "NO" to violence. Mother Teresa of Calcutta is a good example of a non-violent attitude. This story was told in our parish on a Sunday Mass. So, I am not certain of the source.

> Mother Teresa was moving around begging for food for her orphans with her companions. She approached a businessman who was well known to be a miser. When she asked for help, this man spat into her hands and mocked her. People who were with her were angry and wanted to beat up the man. But Mother Teresa calmed them down and smiled at the man with a forgiving spirit, saying: "What you gave me just now was for me, thanks. But now I want you to give something to my children who are in need." On hearing this, the man was ashamed and apologized to Mother Teresa. He never stopped providing for the orphans under the care of Mother Teresa and her Sisters.

Love, they say, conquers hatred. It was the love and kind words that Mother Teresa showed to this miser that transformed him. If the forces of love can meet with violence, then our world will become a better place to reside. Certainly, non-violence and kind words can transform an enemy into a friend.

This work has examined the different faces of violence in our society and how a woman's body is sometimes treated as an object to be used. When one gender dominates and oppresses another, then the system needs to change. Following this line of argument, the African patriarchal society needs transformation. Many women have suffered abuse at home and in society. Often removed from decisions that affect them, these women live with false stories because of violence at home – psychological, sexual, physical, cultural, and economic abuse.

Using the work of Robert Schreiter, this work explains the relationship between violence and reconciliation, how violence changes a victim's true story to a false one, and how the reconciliation process can help a victim redeem her true narrative. This work regards ineffective reconciliation as a hasty peace, reconciliation as a prerequisite to liberation, and reconciliation as a managed process. These inadequate models rendered reconciliation a skill learned rather than what God does. Certainly, through the grace of God, the reconciliation process starts with the victim of violence. However, the Church must create certain conditions before reconciliation can take place. These conditions at the local level include interpreting and using specific gospel passages that refute domestic abuse, emphasizing the recent documents of the Church that promote the dignity of women and family life values, and forming parish support groups to allow victims of abuse to experience healing through rituals, prayers, sharing of stories, seminars, and workshops. Through the support group, the Church listens with compassion to the predicaments of a wounded woman, mourns with her, and empowers her to discard her false story. Through the broken body of Christ in the Eucharist and the rituals of reconciliation, the victim of violence may receive healing in order to rebuild her shattered life.

On a broader, more national level, the African bishops could write and circulate pastoral letters that recognize and condemn domestic abuse as a sin. The bishops could also propose another special prayer against domestic abuse to be said after Sunday Masses in parishes. This new prayer must condemn domestic abuse as a sin and include a petition for forgiveness and healing. All these avenues are aimed at educating the Christian communities to recognize and condemn domestic abuse so that many women who are victimized may be liberated and healed. The recommendations and the process of true reconciliation enumerated in this work are not the only methods for the grace of reconciliation process to take place; however, they can be effective and fruitful in giving voice to the voiceless, liberation to the oppressed, and healing to the wounded women who are seeking for redeemed stories.

Bibliography

Achebe, Chinua. *Things Fall Apart*. New York, NY: Alfred Knopf, Inc., 1992.

Agbasiere, Joseph Thérése. *Women in Igbo Life and Thought*. Edited by Shirley Ardener. New York, NY: Routledge, 2000.

Albom, Mitch. *Tuesdays with Morrie*. New York: Doubleday, 1997.

Amadi, Elechi. *The Concubine*. London: Heinemann Educational Books, 1966.

Ameh, Ebere. "A Walk against Domestic Violence." *The Guardian*, September 10, 2011.

Andolsen, Barbara H. "Whose Sexuality? Whose Tradition? Women, Experience and Roman Catholic Sexual Ethics." In *Readings in Moral Theology, No. 9: Feminist Ethics and the Catholic Moral Tradition*, edited by Charles Curran, Margaret Farley, and Richard McCormick, 207-239. New York, NY: Paulist Press, 1996.

ArtMatters.Info, "Love Charms in Modern Urban Homes," posted 28 September 2008, www.artmatters.info/heritage-formerly-culture/2008/09/love-charms- in-modern-urban-homes

Bellows, Thomas. *Happiness in the Family: Using Choice Theory to Eliminate Hostility in the Family*. Lincoln, NE: iUniverse Inc, 2007.

Bergant,Dianne, and Richard Fragomeni. *Preaching the New Lectionary: Year A*. Collegeville, MN: The Liturgical Press, 2001.

Catholic Bishops Conference of Nigeria. *Restoring the Dignity of the Nigerian Woman*. Lagos, Nigeria: Sovereign Ventures, 2002.

———. "Towards Sustaining our Democracy," Catholic Online, September 25, 2006. http://www.cathoilc.org/national/national_story.php?id=21375.

De Silva, Ranjan. *A Better Way to Sell: Mastery of Sales Through Mastery of Self.* India: Dorling Kindersley Ltd, 2009.

Eastern and Central Africa Women in Development Network. "Violence Against Women: Trainers' Manual." Nairobi, Kenya: Paulines Publications Africa, 2011.

Edet, Rosemary. "Christianity and African Women's Rituals." In *The Will To Arise: Women, Tradition, and the Church in Africa*, edited by Mercy Oduyoye and Musimbi Kanyoro, 25-39. Maryknoll, NY: Orbis Books, 1997.

Engler, Barbara. *Personality Theories*, 9th Edition. Belmont, CA: Cengage Learning Publishers, 2013.

Ezeigbo, Akachi. *The Last of the Strong Ones.* Lagos, Nigeria: Vista Books, 1998.

Fallon, Michael. *The Gospel According to Matthew: An Introduction Commentary.* Bangalore, India: Asian Trading Corporation, 2002.

FIDA-Kenya, "Assessment of the Implementation of the Previous Concluding Observations on Kenya (CCPR/CO/83/KEN) at the time of the Review of the Third Periodic Report," Office of the High Commissioner for Human Rights, Nairobi, Kenya, August 5, 2011 www2.ohchr.org/English/bodies/hrc/docs/ngos/FIDA_Kenya103.doc

Flannery, Austin, ed. *Gaudium et spes*, Vatican Council II, The Conciliar and Post Conciliar Documents. Boston, MA: St. Paul Books and Media, 1992.

Giblin, Marie. "Catholic Church Teaching and Domestic Violence." *Listening: Journal of Religion and Culture*, no. 34 (Jan 1999): 10-21.

Glendon, Mary Ann. "Opening Address at the UN Conference on Women," Eternal Word Television Network, September 5, 1995. http://www.ewtn.com/library/CURIA/STATBEIJ.HTM.

Grayson, Stuart. *Spiritual Healing: A Simple Guide for the Healing of the Body, Mind and Spirit.* New York, NY: Simon & Schuster, 1997.

Gupte, Deepak. *Wisdom 101: The Best Gift You Can Give Yourself.* Bloomington, IN: Xlibris Corporation, 2009.

Igbuku, Augustine. *The Pursuit of Sterling Attitude.* Oxford, UK: PubliciseJesus, 2015.

Igwemezie, Regina. "Widowhood: A Harrowing Experience," Unpublished Monograph, ISBN: 978-2643-96-13 Anambra, Nigeria: 2005.

Ilogu, Edmund. *Christianity and Ibo Culture.* Leiden Netherlands: E.J. Brill, 1974.

John Paul II. *Familiaris consortio*, Libreria Editrice Vaticana, December 15, 1981. http://www.vatican.va/holy_father/john_paul_ii/apost_exhortations/documents/hf_jp-ii_exh_19811122_familiaris-consortio_en.html.

_____. "Letter of John Paul II to Women," Libreria Editrice Vaticana, June 29, 1995. http://www.vatican.va/holy_father/john_paul_ii/letters/documents/hf_jp-ii_let_29061995_ women _en.html, no. 3.

_____. "Mulieris dignitatem," Libreria Editrice Vaticana, August 15, 1988. www.vatican.va/holy_father/john_paul_ii/apost_

letters/documents/hf_jp-ii_apl_15081988_mulieria-dignitatem_en.html.

―――――. "Theology of the Body," Eternal Word Television Network, August 25, 1982. www.ewtn.com/library/papaldoc/jp2tbind.htm.

Kelly, Liz. May Crowing, *Mass and Merton: And Other Reasons I Love Being Catholic*. Chicago, IL: Loyola Press, 2006.

Kroeger, Catherine, and Mary Evans, eds. *IVP Women's Bible Commentary*, (Downers Grove, IL: Intervarsity Press, 2002), 517-546.

Lafraniere, Sharon. "Entrenched Epidemic: Wife Beatings in Africa." *New York Times*, August 11, 2005.

Law, Lois. "Implementation of the Domestic Violence Act 116 of 1998," South African Catholic Bishop's Conference Parliamentary Liaison Office, October 16, 2009. http://d2zmx6mlqh7g3a.doudfront.net/cdn/farfuture/mtime:1259069738/files/docs/091028sacbc_0.pdf

Majtenyi Report, "Cases of Domestic Violence Increase in Kenya." Voice of America, March 4, 2010, www.voanews.com/content/cases-of-domestic-violence-increase-in-kenya-86691287/113574.html

Mathai, A. Muthoni. *Sexual Decision-making and AIDS in Africa: A Look at the Social Vulnerability of Women in Sub-Saharan Africa to HIV/AIDS: A Kenyan Example*. Kassel, Germany: Kassel University Press, 2006.

Means, Jeffrey. *Trauma and Evil: Healing the Wounded Soul*. Minneapolis, MN: Augsburg Fortress, 2000.

Moloney, Francis. *The Gospel of John, Sacra Pagina Series*, Vol. 4, edited by Daniel Harrington Collegeville, MN: The Liturgical Press, 1998.

Murphy, Tim, and Loriann Oberlin. *Overcoming Passive-Aggression: How to Stop Hidden Anger from Spoiling your Relationships, Career and Happiness.* Cambridge, MA: Da Capo Press, 2005.

Mwau, Angellina. "Counseling Victims of Domestic Violence in Kenya." In *African Women's Health*, edited by Meredeth Turshen, 107-124. Asmara, Eritrea: Africa World Press, 2000.

Naylor, Nikki. "Drafting Domestic Violence Legislation in Nigeria: Lessons from South Africa." Women's Legal Centre (September 2005): 1-34.

Nwachukwu-Udaku, Benedict. *From What We Should Do To Who We Should Be: Negotiating Theological Reflections and Praxis in the Context of HIV/ AIDS Among the Igbos of Nigeria.* Bloomington, IN: Author House, 2011.

Nwankwoala, Celestina. *A Letter to my Countrymen.* (Bloomington, IN: AuthorHouse, 2013), 52.

Obioma, Des-Obi, and Boniface Ogbenna, "Women Issues: Violence Against Women in Africa: An Exposition." In *The Kpim of Feminism: Issues and Women in a Changing World*, edited by George U Ukagba, Des-obi Obioma, and Iks Nwankwor, 328-338. Victoria BC, Canada: Trafford, 2010.

O'Day, Gail. "John." In *Women's Bible Commentary*, edited by Carol Newsom and Sharon Ringe, 381-393. Louisville, KY: Westminster John Knox Press, 1998.

Oduor, Peter. "A Drink, a Pill, and Lots of Tears: Inside Kenya's Silent Epidemic of Drugging, Raping, and Dumping." *Daily Kenya Living 2, Daily Nation* (July 2, 2013): 2-6.

Oduyoye, Mercy A. *Daughters of Anowa: African Women and Patriarchy.* Maryknoll, NY: Orbis Books, 1995.

_____. *Introducing African Women's Theology.* Cleveland, OH: The Pilgrim Press, 2001.

Okoh, Michael. *Fostering Christian Faith in Schools and Christian Communities through Igbo Traditional Values: Towards a Holistic Approach to Christian Religious Education and Catechesis in Igboland.* Berlin, Germany: Lit VerLag, 2012.

Okoye, Justina. "Gender Violence: A Comparative Study of Mariama Mâ's Un Chant écarlate and Theodora Akachi Ezeigbo's The Last of the Strong Ones." In T*he Kpim of Feminism Issues and Women in a Changing World*, edited by George U Ukagba, Des-obi Obioma, and Iks Nwankwor, 356-363. Victoria BC, Canada: Trafford, 2010.

Okpalaenwe, N. Elizabeth. *The Power to Succeed.* Menji, Cameroon: ANU-CAM, 2005.

_____. *Psychological Counselling for Africa: Handbook on Psychotherapy and Cultural Counselling in African Contexts.* Nigeria, Onitsha: Laurans Prints, 2014.

Ose, Ailie. "Prevalence of Domestic Violence in Nigeria: Implications for Counseling." *Edo Journal of Counseling* 2, no. 1 (May 2009): 1-8.

Oyediran, Kolawole, and Uche Isiugo-Abanihe. "Perceptions of Nigerian Women on Domestic Violence: Evidence from 2003

Nigeria Demographic and Health Survey." *African Journal of Reproductive Health* 9, no. 2 (August 2005): 38-53.

Pazdan, Mary Margaret. *Becoming God's Beloved in the Company of Friends: A Spirituality of the Fourth Gospel*. Eugene, OR: Cascade Books, 2007.

Poling, James. "Male Violence Against Women and Children." In *The Care of Men*, edited by Christie C. Neuger and James N. Poling, 138-162. Nashville, TN: Abingdon Press, 1997.

_____. "Preaching to Perpetrators of Violence." In *Telling the Truth: Preaching about Sexual and Domestic Violence*, edited by John McClure and Nancy Ramsay, 71-82. Cleveland, OH: United Church Press, 1998.

Reid, Barbara. "Sabbath, the Crown of Creation." In *Earth, Wind, and Fire: Biblical and Theological Perspectives on Creation*, edited by Carol Dempsey and Mary Margaret Pazdan, 67-76. Collegeville, MN: Liturgical Press, 2004.

Restifo, Francesca, et al., *Violence Against Women and Children in Kenya: An Alternative Report to the Committee Against Torture*. Geneva, Switzerland: World Organization Against Torture, 2009.

Saibil, Diane. "SSRI Antidepressant: Their Place in Women's Lives" *Women and Health Protection*, www.whp-apsf.ca/en/documents/ssri.html

Schreiter Robert. *In Water and In Blood: A Spirituality of Solidarity and Hope*. NY: Crossroad, 1988.

_____. "Liturgy as Reconciling." *Liturgical Ministry* 17, no. 3 (Sum 2008): 139-145.

_____. *Reconciliation: Mission and Ministry in a Changing Social Order.* Maryknoll, NY: Orbis Books, 1992.

_____. "Reconciliation and Healing as a Paradigm for Mission." *International Review of Mission* 94, (Jan 2005): 74-83.

_____. "Reconciliation as a Missionary Task." *Missiology* 20, no.1 (Jan 1992): 3-10.

_____. *The Ministry of Reconciliation: Spirituality and Strategies.* Maryknoll, NY: Orbis Books, 1998.

_____. "The Ministry of Forgiveness in a Praxis of Reconciliation." An International Seminar on Reconciliation, Lima, Peru: August 21, 2006, preciousbloodspirituality.org/spirituality-and-theology/ ministry-forgiveness-and-praxis-reconciliation.

The Herald. November 24, 2014, "He Threatens to Kill Me, Woman Tells Court" (https://www.herald.co.zw/he-threatens-to-kill-me-woman-tells-court).

Uchem, Rose. *Overcoming Women's Subordination in the Igbo African Culture and in the Catholic Church: Envisioning an Inclusive Theology with Reference to Women.* Enugu, Nigeria: Snaap Press, 2001.

United States Conference of Catholic Bishops, "When I Call for Help: A Pastoral Response to Domestic Violence Against Women." November 12, 2002, https:// www.usccb.org/laity/help.shtml.

www.ingramcontent.com/pod-product-compliance
Lightning Source LLC
LaVergne TN
LVHW020929090426
835512LV00020B/3286